Macdonald
Educational

The

The author wishes to thank Dr Brian
Dobson of Durham University and Mr H
Russell Robinson of the Tower of London
for their advice and help in checking
the manuscript and illustrations. He
would also like to thank Dr Valerie
Maxfield for her help with pages 68–9.

The measurements in this book are
metric. There is a conversion table at
the end of the book after the index.
Where miles or feet are mentioned in the
text, these refer to the Roman
measurements. These are slightly
shorter than modern miles and feet.

First published 1975
Third reprint 1978
Macdonald Educational
Holywell House
Worship Street
London EC2A 2EN

Published in the United
States by Silver Burdett
Company, Morristown, N.J.
1979 Printing
Library of Congress
Catalog Card No. 79-65845
ISBN 0-382-06306-6

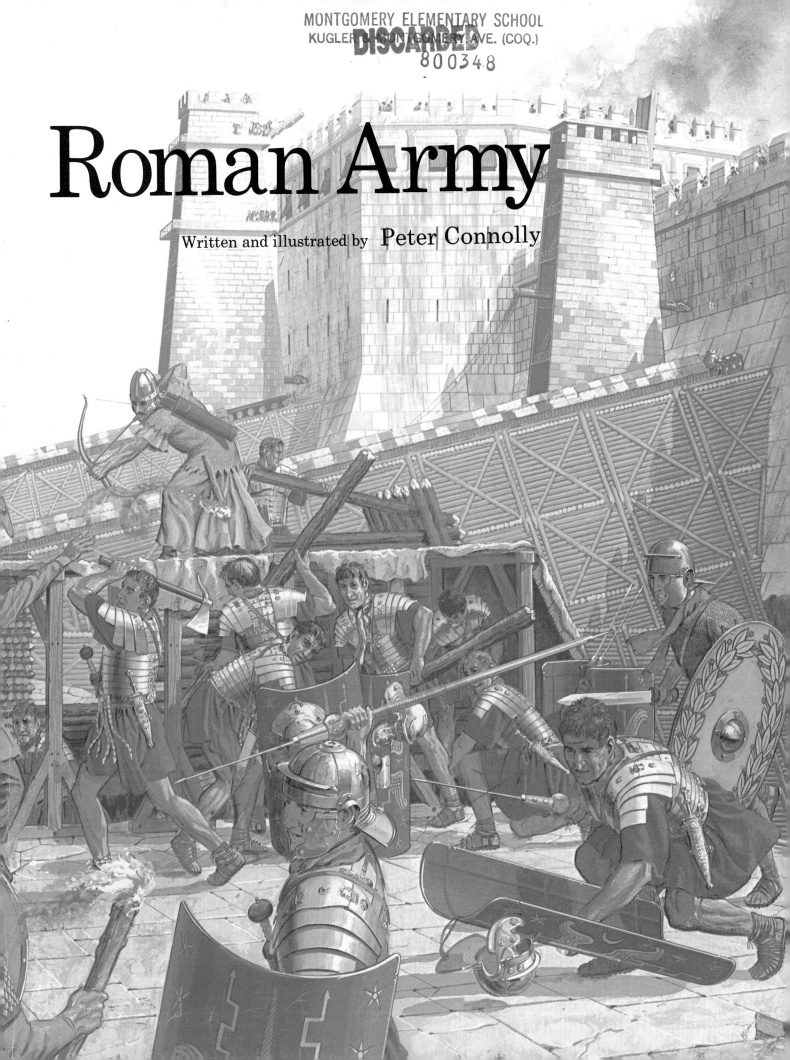

Roman Army

Written and illustrated by **Peter Connolly**

Rome was founded during the European iron age in about 800 BC. Beginning as a small village on the Tiber, she rose to dominate first Italy and finally the whole Mediterranean basin. The conquest of Italy took 600 years; the rest took little over a hundred. How did she achieve such remarkable success?

This book provides an account of the Roman Army during three critically important periods: the Macedonian campaign, Caesar's conquest of northern Europe, and the early years of the Empire. The text at the top of each page gives an exciting narrative of events, whilst the illustrations and text below vividly depict the armour, tactics, weapons and organization of the legions as they evolved.

In the 2nd century BC, Rome was a republic. She had already completed her conquest of Italy and controlled Spain and north-west Africa. Her main rivals, Carthage and Syria, had been defeated. Only the Greek state of Macedonia remained defiant. The first section of this book describes the victory over Macedonia which left Rome the undisputed master of the Mediterranean world.

Our second section deals with the army of Caesar's time, in the middle of the 1st century BC. By now the legions had been reorganized. A new type of army came into being, loyal not to Rome but to its military leaders.

Finally, we proceed to an analysis of the army of the early Empire, during the 1st century AD. Rome had now created a single political unit that stretched from Scotland in the north to Egypt in the south, from Spain in the west to Armenia in the east. But the period was marred by violent civil warfare. The army which had achieved so much was convulsed with internal strife, as different legions competed to put their own commanders on the imperial throne. The story of this struggle unfolds in the third section of the book which ends with the fall of Jerusalem in AD 70.

Roman Army

CONTENTS

8   The Army of the Republic

10   *The Legions*

12   *Marching and Camping*

14   *The Camp*

16   *The Battle*

18   *Armour and Weapons of the Republic*

20   *The Navy: the Rise of Roman Sea Power*

22   *The Navy: War Galleys*

24   The Army at the Time of Caesar

26   *The New Legions*

28   *Military Engineering: Bridges*

30   *Military Engineering: Roads and Ramps*

32   *Blockades*

34   *Armour and Weapons of Caesar's Time*

36   The Army of the Empire

38   *The Frontiers*

40   *The Legions of the Empire*

42   *Praetorian and Urban Cohorts*

44   *The Life of a Legionary*

46   *The Officers*

48   *Legionary Armour*

50   *Legionary Equipment*

52   *On the March*

54   *Auxiliary Infantry*

56   *Frontier Defences*

58   *The Cavalry*

60   *Cavalry Equipment*

62   *Siege Tactics and Equipment*

64   *Parades and Sports*

66   *Siege Weapons: Rams and Catapults*

68   *Rewards and Punishments*

70   *Triumph and Ovation*

72   *The Triumph of Titus*

74   Glossary

76   Index

The Army of the Republic

On 22nd June, 168 BC, the Roman Army finally managed to precipitate a full scale battle with the forces of Macedon after three years of fruitless campaigning.

The legendary Macedonian phalanx was cut to pieces at Pydna in Greece, beneath the craggy heights of Mount Olympus. So came to an end the kingdom of Alexander the Great which had once held sway over an empire stretching from Greece to India.

After the fall of Macedon, Rome took hostages from those Greek states which had opposed her, as a guarantee for their good behaviour. Among these hostages was a young man called Polybius, who came from Megalopolis in Achaea. It is lucky for us that this young man was not only interested in military affairs but that he spent his years of bondage in the house of Scipio Aemilianus, the son of the conqueror of Macedonia, and accompanied him on his campaigns.

Polybius wrote a history of the Greco-Roman world with particular emphasis on military matters. He is considered one of the most reliable of the ancient historians. Armed with his account and with the results of the excavations at Numantia in Spain, where Aemilianus conducted a long drawn-out siege, we are able to piece together a fairly accurate account of the Roman Army at this period in the Republic's history.

Left : At the Battle of Pydna, the Roman legionaries broke through the rigid mass of pikes of the Macedonian phalanx. The Roman swordsmen then cut the Macedonian spearmen to pieces.

The Legions

The war with Macedonia had dragged on for three years when Aemilius Paullus was elected one of the two consuls for the year 168 BC. He was given the task of bringing the war to a quick end.

Paullus had under his command two 5,000-strong legions plus a similar number of men supplied by the cities of Italy allied to Rome. He had a total of 20,000 infantry, 2,500 cavalry and about 34 elephants. Elephants were seldom used by Rome. In this case they were used to strengthen the cavalry.

Before setting out for Greece, Paullus appointed

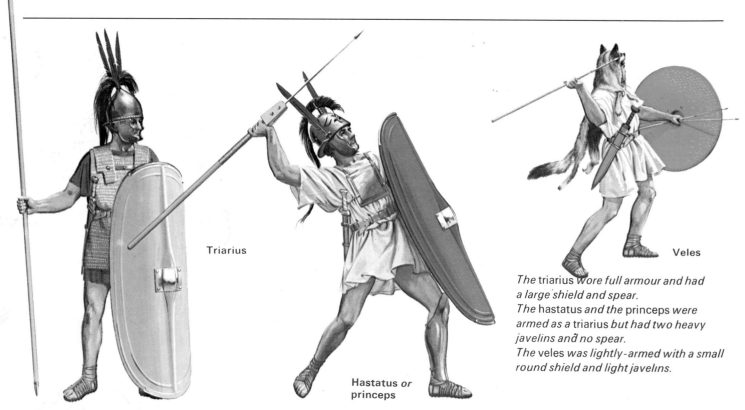

Triarius

Hastatus *or* princeps

Veles

The triarius *wore full armour and had a large shield and spear.*
The hastatus *and the* princeps *were armed as a* triarius *but had two heavy javelins and no spear.*
The veles *was lightly-armed with a small round shield and light javelins.*

The levy

At the beginning of each year, two consuls were elected. The new consuls' first task was to appoint their staff officers (tribunes). The tribunes had to enrol sufficient recruits to bring the legions up to strength.

On a certain day, all property-owning Roman citizens between 17 and 46 were assembled on the Capitoline Hill.

Here they were arranged by height and age. They were then brought forward four at a time to be selected for service in the legions. The tribunes of each legion took it in turns to have first choice. In this way they ensured an even distribution of experience and quality throughout the forces.

The new recruits then swore the oath of obedience. It was sworn in full by one man and the others said *"Idem in me"* (the same for me).

The legionaries

There were four types of legionary. *Hastati* and *principes* were soldiers in the prime of life. They formed the main strength of the legion. They wore full armour and carried a sword and two long javelins (*pila*) one light and one heavy. The *hastati* formed the front line and the *principes* the second.

Triarii were the veteran soldiers of the army. Although they wore the same armour as the *hastati* and *principes*, they carried a long spear instead of javelins. These men formed the rear rank but were seldom brought into battle. A Roman expression "the battle came to the *triarii*" was used to describe a desperate situation.

Velites were skirmishers. They were armed only with helmet and shield. Their offensive weapons were the sword and short javelins.

The legions

The army normally consisted of four legions but in an emergency it might be many times this number. In the war against Hannibal (218–202 BC) there were even two legions of freed slaves.

The normal legion strength was 4,200 but it was sometimes increased to about 5,000. During this period a legion always means one legion plus an equal number of allies.

The legion was divided into 60 units called centuries. These centuries were coupled in pairs called maniples. The *hastati*, *principes* and *triarii* were each divided into ten maniples. The *velites* were distributed among these.

Each legion also had 300 cavalry. These were selected from the wealthiest citizens.

his staff officers (tribunes). The job of bringing the legions up to strength fell to these men. On an appointed day, all Romans eligible for service were assembled on the Capitoline Hill. Here the tribunes selected the men required to swell the ranks.

Recruiting officers were also sent to the allied cities of Italy so that their contingents might be brought up to strength too. The new recruits were given a date by which they must report to their legions and were then dismissed.

On arrival at the camp in Greece the new recruits, most of whom had seen service before, were posted to their centuries. The poorest and youngest recruits joined the skirmishers. Those in the prime of manhood were posted to the heavy infantry and the oldest joined the rearguard.

With the army now up to strength, Paullus set about his task. The Macedonian army, headed by the young king, Perseus, was strongly entrenched near Mount Olympus on the east coast of Greece. Communications with Macedonia to the north were good by both land and sea and the previous Roman consul had not succeeded in any of his attempts to force a battle.

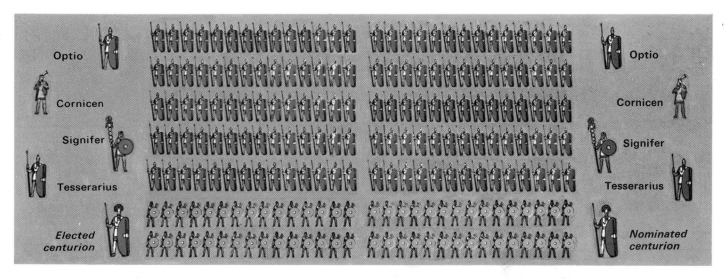

The officers

To command the maniples, the legion elected 30 centurions. Each of these nominated a second centurion. Each centurion chose a second-in-command (*optio*) and the other officers for his century: a standard bearer (*signifer*), trumpeter (*cornicen*) and a *tesserarius* who each night received the password written on a tablet (*tessera*).

The elected centurion was the senior centurion of the maniple and he commanded the right-hand century.

The first centurion elected (*primus pilus*) was the highest-ranking centurion. The overall command was entrusted to six tribunes who received their orders from the consul.

The allies

The cities allied to Rome were bound to supply a similar number of soldiers. These were organized in the same way as the legions. Because of the weakness of the Roman cavalry, the allies supplied three times the number of horsemen.

One-fifth of the infantry and one-third of the cavalry were set aside for special duty. These were called *extraordinarii*.

Above: A maniple of hastati/principes consisted of 120–150 heavily-armed javelineers and 50–60 velites. It was organized into two centuries, each

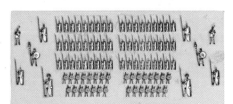

Above: A maniple of triarii was always 60 veteran spearmen with a number of velites organized into two centuries commanded as the hastati/principes.

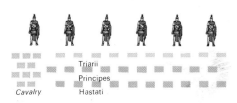

Above: A legion composed of 10 maniples of hastati, 10 maniples of principes, 10 maniples of triarii and 10 turmae of cavalry. The whole legion was commanded by six tribunes.

commanded by a centurion and his optio, with a standard bearer, trumpeter and guard commander (tesserarius).

Above: A turma of cavalry: 30 horsemen in three squadrons, each commanded by a decurion and his optio. A cavalryman was liable to 10 years service.

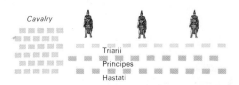

Above: A contingent of allies composed of 30 infantry maniples, as in the legion, and 30 turmae of cavalry. The command was held by three praefecti nominated by the consul.

Marching and Camping

Macedonians are forced to break camp

By a circuitous march of his *extraordinarii*, Paullus managed to cut Perseus's land communications. The navy did the same at sea. The Roman consul then mounted a series of blistering attacks on the Macedonian camp. Perseus became convinced that his position was no longer safe. Under cover of darkness, he broke camp and withdrew northwards.

The legions followed at dawn the following morning. By mid-morning the scouts had informed the consul that they were approaching the new Macedonian position to the north-east of Mount

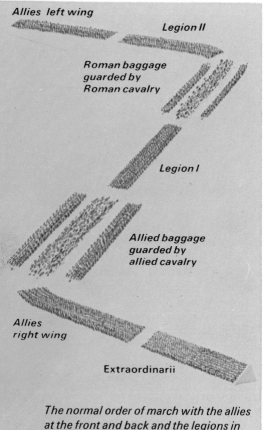

Allies left wing

Legion II

Roman baggage guarded by Roman cavalry

Legion I

Allied baggage guarded by allied cavalry

Allies right wing

Extraordinarii

The normal order of march with the allies at the front and back and the legions in the centre. The cavalry covers the baggage train.

In hostile country the legions could advance in battle order with the baggage between the files.

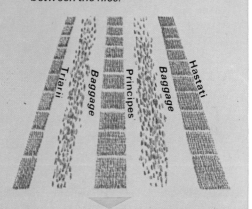

Triarii — Baggage — Principes — Baggage — Hastati

Breaking camp

On the first trumpet blast, the tents of the consuls and tribunes were struck. The soldiers then took down their own. On a second signal they packed them onto the mules and on the third, the vanguard set out from the camp.

Marching

The *extraordinarii* normally formed the vanguard unless there was fear of attack from behind. In this case they would take up the rearguard position. Then came the right wing of the allies, followed by the two legions. The rear was brought up by the left wing of the allies. The cavalry might either accompany their infantry units or cover the flanks of the baggage train.

When the army was marching through open hostile country, the infantry divided into *hastati*, *principes* and *triarii* and marched in three parallel columns with the baggage train in between the files. The whole army could more easily then form their battle-line if an attack took place.

Pitching camp

A tribune was sent ahead of the army to find a suitable site for the camp. He would look for a site about 800 metres square, preferably on raised ground. The site should not offer cover to an attacking enemy and had to be near water.

The tribune planted a white flag to mark the site of the consul's tent, the *praetorium*, at the best vantage point. Red flags were planted at other points to show where the officers and legionaries were to camp.

At the centre of the line marked out for the legionaries' tents, the tribune set up his surveying instrument (*groma*) to measure out the camp. He marked the line of the frontal defences of the camp at a distance of 400 metres. The tribune

An Etruscan cornu *(horn)* 4th-3rd century BC

also marked out with spears the line of the three main streets. One ran from the *praetorium* through the middle of the camp, and the other two crossed it at right angles.

When the enemy was nearby, the baggage train was placed behind the lines marked out for the frontal defences of the camp. The *velites*, the cavalry and half of the heavy infantry, drawn up in battle array, were placed in front of the line. Behind this human rampart, the other half of the infantry set to work throwing up the defences.

The legionaries dug a trench three metres deep and four metres wide. The earth from this ditch was piled up on the side nearest the *praetorium* and flattened off along the top at a height of about $1\frac{1}{4}$ metres. The front of this mound was faced with turf from the ditch.

Above: *The* groma, *the ancient surveying instrument. This instrument enabled the surveyor to lay out a rectangular grid. It has been reconstructed from remains found at Pompeii.*

Olympus. Paullus dispatched one of the tribunes with a small detachment to survey the area for a suitable camp site. The tribune found a low spur of rising ground, watered by a small stream, about a mile from the enemy camp. An area of about 800 metres square was cleared and the camp marked out.

It was mid-day by the time that the army reached the site. The soldiers were eager for battle but they could hardly fight their best after a forced march through the heat of the day. Paullus decided to entrench. While part of his army faced the enemy, the rest dug the fortifications for the camp.

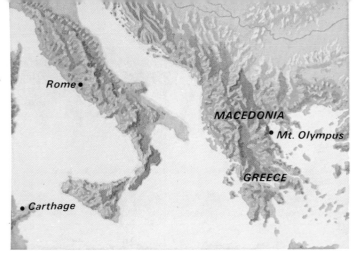

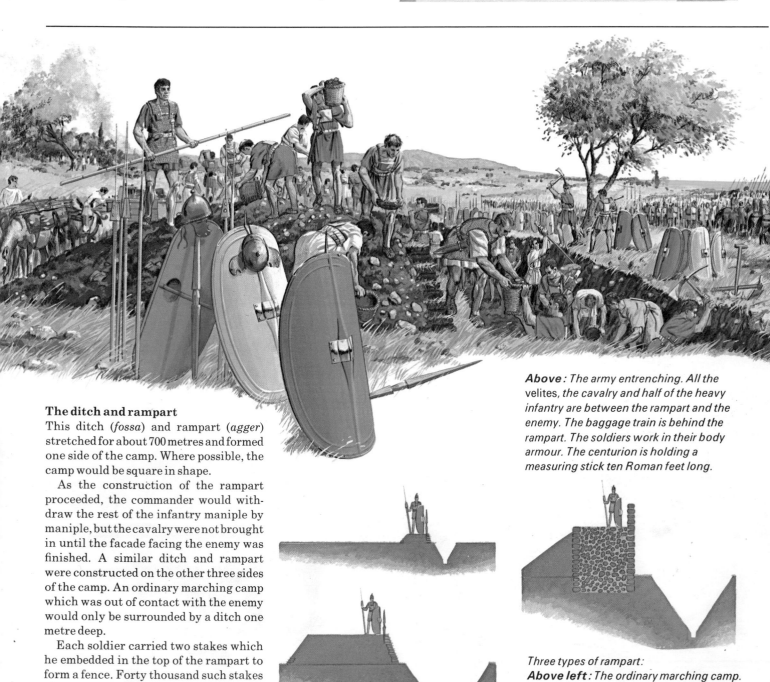

The ditch and rampart

This ditch (*fossa*) and rampart (*agger*) stretched for about 700 metres and formed one side of the camp. Where possible, the camp would be square in shape.

As the construction of the rampart proceeded, the commander would withdraw the rest of the infantry maniple by maniple, but the cavalry were not brought in until the facade facing the enemy was finished. A similar ditch and rampart were constructed on the other three sides of the camp. An ordinary marching camp which was out of contact with the enemy would only be surrounded by a ditch one metre deep.

Each soldier carried two stakes which he embedded in the top of the rampart to form a fence. Forty thousand such stakes placed on a rampart with a 3,000 metre circuit would make about 13 to a metre. The stakes were tied together at the centre.

Above: The army entrenching. All the velites, the cavalry and half of the heavy infantry are between the rampart and the enemy. The baggage train is behind the rampart. The soldiers work in their body armour. The centurion is holding a measuring stick ten Roman feet long.

Three types of rampart:
Above left: The ordinary marching camp.
Left: The marching camp in the face of the enemy.
Above: A stone rampart from Numantia, Spain.

The Camp

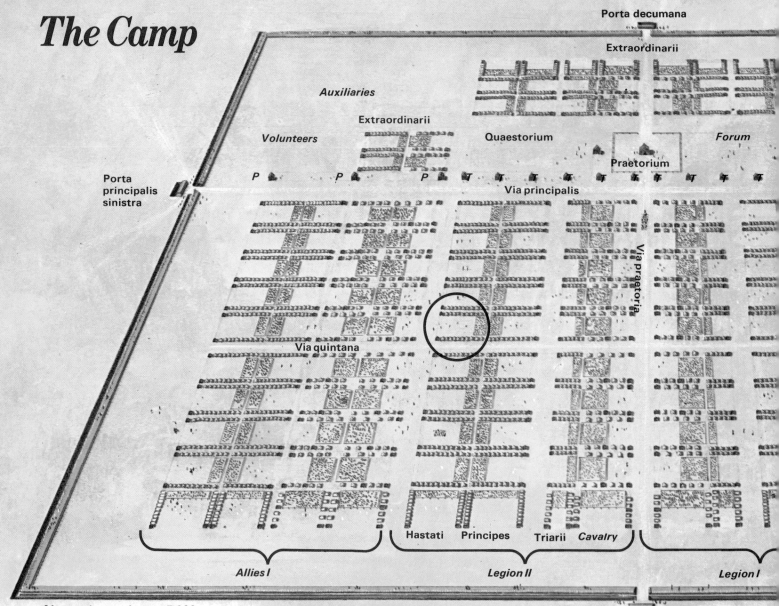

Porta decumana

Extraordinarii

Auxiliaries

Volunteers

Extraordinarii

Quaestorium

Forum

Praetorium

Porta
principalis
sinistra

P   P   P T   T   T   T   T   T   T   T

Via principalis

Via praetoria

Via quintana

Hastati   Principes   Triarii   *Cavalry*

Allies I

Legion II

Legion I

Porta praetoria

Above: A camp for two 5,000-strong legions, as described by Polybius. It was about 800 metres square. There were three main streets and four exits. The job of guarding these exits fell to the velites *who were quartered with their maniples. Other guard duties were performed by the heavy infantry.*

Below: Types of tent as shown on Trajan's Column.

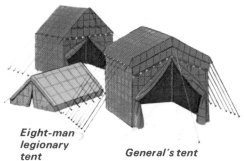

Officer's tent

Eight-man legionary tent

General's tent

The camp

The camp was formed within the entrenched area. Since the layout of the camp was always the same, every unit knew exactly where to pitch its tents. An empty space about 70 metres wide was left just inside the rampart so that any missiles coming over the defences would not reach the tents. The occupied area was laid out like a town with streets and a market place (*forum*).

The *tesserarii* of each maniple had to report to the *praetorium* at dusk when the password was handed out.

The duty officer was selected from the cavalry. Accompanied by two companions, he made his rounds to inspect the guard at night. During one such inspection, some of the heavy infantry guards were found asleep, propped up by their javelins, with their chins resting on the top of their large oval shields. The usual punishment for this was being beaten or stoned, often to death, by the comrades whose lives had been put at risk.

Marching camps had no gates. Certain types of ramparts were used at the entrances. These would not necessarily keep the enemy out but they did prevent them from charging the entrances.

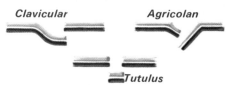

Clavicular   *Agricolan*

Tutulus

Above: Three main types of camp entrance. The bank is light and the ditch is dark brown.

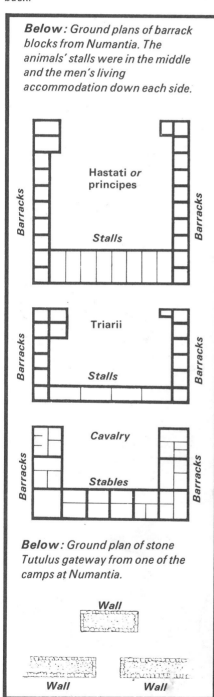

Above: Reconstruction of a maniple block from a semi-permanent camp at Numantia in Spain. The legionaries are billeted along the sides with the centurions at the nearest end. The baggage animals are stalled across the back.

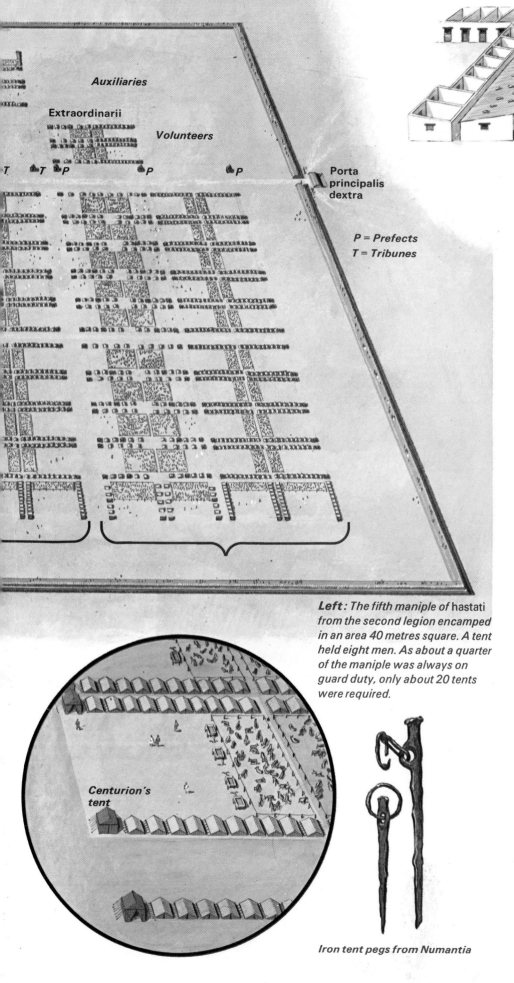

Auxiliaries

Extraordinarii

Volunteers

T   T   P   P   P

Porta
principalis
dextra

P = Prefects
T = Tribunes

Left: The fifth maniple of hastati from the second legion encamped in an area 40 metres square. A tent held eight men. As about a quarter of the maniple was always on guard duty, only about 20 tents were required.

Centurion's tent

Iron tent pegs from Numantia

Below: Ground plans of barrack blocks from Numantia. The animals' stalls were in the middle and the men's living accommodation down each side.

Barracks

Hastati *or* principes

Stalls

Barracks

Barracks

Triarii

Stalls

Barracks

Barracks

Cavalry

Stables

Barracks

Below: Ground plan of stone Tutulus gateway from one of the camps at Numantia.

Wall

Wall   Wall

The Battle

The following morning a skirmish broke out between the opposing watering parties. The Macedonians, now eager for battle, called out their whole force and advanced towards the Roman camp. Paullus immediately sent out the cavalry and *velites* to slow them down. He then led out the legions and drew them up in battle array. At the sound of the trumpets, the cavalry and *velites* withdrew to their positions and the massed legions moved forward.

As the two armies closed, the legionaries threw their *pila* (heavy javelins) and then charged in with

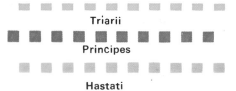

Above: A Roman army drawn up in battle order with the two legions in the centre flanked by the allies and with the cavalry on the wings.

Triarii

Principes

Hastati

Above: When drawn up in battle order, the maniples were spaced out to leave a maniple's width between each. The principes *covered the spaces between the* hastati *maniples and the* triarii *covered those between the* principes *maniples.*

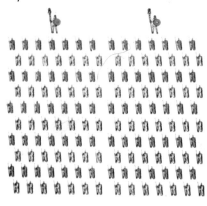

Above: A maniple of the principes/ hastati *in open order.*
Below: The same maniple in closed order.

9+10
7+8
5+6
3+4
1+2

The battle array

The normal battle array was composed of two Roman legions in the centre, flanked by two allied legions. The cavalry was placed on the wings.

The *hastati* formed the front rank arranged in their maniples, with a space equivalent to a maniple between each. Behind these spaces the maniples of *principes* were drawn up. At the rear were the *triarii*, likewise covering the spaces between the *principes*.

The maniples were formed up with the senior centurion on the right and the junior on the left. The two standard bearers might often be at the front of the charge but they would usually stand behind the last rank of their century during the fighting.

Open and closed ranks

The legionaries were probably drawn up in the same way as the maniples, with each rank covering the spaces in the rank in front.

Ordinarily there was a space of two metres between legionaries but a tighter formation could be formed by advancing the even ranks into the spaces in the rank in front. The legionaries probably charged in open order and closed ranks after they had thrown their *pila*.

The number of ranks in the maniple would usually be governed by the formation of the enemy, the maniples being sufficiently deep to withstand the enemy charge. The most common depth seems to have been about eight ranks in open order or four ranks in closed order. At the Battle of Pydna the maniples were probably very deep to match the density of the Macedonian formation.

The start of the battle

Before offering battle, the commander would call his priests to tell him whether the omens were favourable. He would

then normally address his troops to encourage them to fight well. The battle would be started by the *velites* and the cavalry, who would harass the enemy and try to shake their confidence.

When the legions were ready to advance a trumpet signal was given. The *velites* would withdraw through the intermanipular spaces to the back of their respective units and the cavalry would withdraw to the wings. Sometimes the *velites* would reinforce the cavalry.

The whole army would then move forward to within the range of the enemy. The *hastati* would advance to within about 20 metres, throwing first their lighter and then their heavier *pila*. If the javelins did not actually hit the enemy, they would often become embedded in the shields, their barbed points making them difficult to withdraw. The long metal shaft was slim and would usually buckle on impact, making it impossible for the enemy to throw it back. If it stuck in his shield, its weight made his shield uncontrollable.

Close quarters

During the confusion caused by this hail of spears, the legionary drew his sword and charged in to close quarters. The *principes*, who were the cream of the army, could now be moved up into the spaces between the *hastati* maniples.

The Macedonian phalanx had been designed to crush any enemy formation by sheer weight. It was composed of about sixteen ranks of pikemen armed with spears about six metres long. The spears of the first five ranks stuck out beyond the front line.

The Roman formation was much lighter and in danger of being forced back by the Macedonian phalanx. The Romans compensated for this lack of weight by their volley of javelins which broke the force of the Macedonian charge.

their swords. The Macedonians lowered their long spears, the points of the first five ranks sticking out beyond the phalanx. The two armies met with a resounding thud as the mass of Greek spears sank deep into the Roman shields, locking the two armies together. There they remained, unable to move.

The uneven pressure along the line and the irregularities of the ground had, as always, opened gaps in the Macedonian phalanx. Seeing this, Paullus gave orders for the maniples to operate independently. From that moment the centurions took over. Wherever there was a space they led their men in, cutting and thrusting at the undefended sides of the Macedonian spearmen. The second legion now threw its whole strength against the centre of the enemy line. The phalanx shuddered and broke under this double assault. The mighty Greek spears were now nothing but an encumbrance and the legionaries closed in for the kill, screaming their war cry. The battle became a massacre.

As the sun set and Olympus cast its long shadows across the battlefield, Paullus called off the pursuit and counted the dead. Of the Romans, one hundred had fallen; of the Macedonians, twenty thousand.

Versatility

The great advantage of the Roman formation was its versatility. Reserves could be brought up wherever needed. The *triarii* were usually held back as a rearguard. At the Battle of Cynoscephalae (197 BC), they were brought up on the wings and attacked the enemy flanks.

If desired, the *principes* could be moved forward into the intervals to form a phalanx. Scipio did the exact opposite at Zama (202 BC) when Hannibal's elephants charged. He moved the *principes* sideways leaving gaps through the legion. The elephants passed through the Roman army and were killed behind the lines.

Battle tactics

The Romans were not great tacticians but relied mainly on the discipline and superior skill of the legionaries. Even bad generals could win battles. The usual aim of the legion was to smash through the centre of the enemy's line shattering both his unity and his morale. This tactic, when practised against a genius such as Hannibal could have disastrous consequences. At Cannae (216 BC) it was the cause of Rome's greatest defeat. Hannibal drew back his centre and charged the Roman wings, thus "rolling up" the Roman Army.

Variations

Only under a brilliant commander, such as Scipio or Caesar, was this tactic varied. Scipio, when fighting Hannibal's brother, held back his centre, attacking both the Carthaginian wings and defeating them before the centres met. (Scipio was present as a youth at Cannae and Hannibal's military genius was not wasted on him.)

The Romans often refined their "smash through the centre" tactic with a wedge formation known to the soldiers as "the pig's head". There was also the square formation which has been used by most armies when surrounded. Occasionally the terrain allowed a commander to vary his tactics but the legionaries' skill was usually the decisive factor.

Above: As the legionary charges he throws first his lighter and then his heavier javelin. He then draws his sword and charges in to close quarters.

Above: By moving the principes *forward into the spaces between the* hastati, *a phalanx could be formed.*

Above: When Hannibal's elephants charged at Zama, Scipio moved his principes *sideways and let the elephants pass straight through the legions.*

Above: At Cynoscephalae the triarii *were brought round to charge the enemy wings.*

Above: To break through the enemy, the maniples could be formed into a wedge nicknamed "the pig's head".

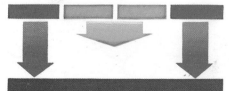

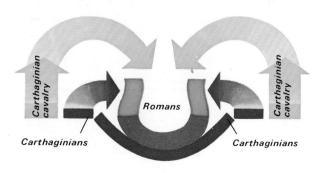

Left: Hannibal's brilliant tactic at Cannae (216 BC). The Romans charged the centre. Hannibal withdrew his centre and charged on the wings. His cavalry completed the encirclement.

Right: Scipio adopts Hannibal's tactic. He withholds his centre and charges on the wings.

Armour and Weapons of the Republic

Armour

After the Battle of Pydna, Paullus set out on a triumphal tour of Greece. At Delphi he erected a monument in marble to his victory at Pydna.

This sculpture is the earliest representation of Roman legionaries. Unfortunately it was painted and the sculptor did not bother to show more than the basic shape of the cuirass, shield, etc.

As on most Roman monuments, the weapons were made of bronze and plugged into holes in the stone. 2,100 years later, no paint or bronze remains, and such is the damage to the stone that no helmet is clearly shown.

Polybius tells us that a poor legionary made do with a small square breast plate; the rich wore a coat of mail. He also tells us that the legionary wore a greave (leg guard). This is confirmed by Arrian who says it was worn on the leading leg. Polybius describes the Roman shield as four Roman feet high, two feet wide and curved. It was made of wood covered with canvas and hide and had an iron boss. The coat of mail and the shield are clearly depicted on the monument at Delphi.

A few metal discs, which are possibly round breast plates, were found at Numantia. Several Italian helmets from the mid to late Republic have also survived and we may be sure that the legionary was similarly armed.

Weapons

During the 3rd century BC the Romans came into contact with Spanish weaponry and were so impressed that they modified many of their own weapons. They even called their sword *gladius hispaniensis* or Spanish sword. The Spanish dagger is also almost identical with later Roman types. Excavations at Numantia have recovered both light and heavy *pilum* heads and the light javelin heads of the *velites*.

Above: Figures from the monument of Aemilius Paullus at Delphi. Like most Roman sculpture it was painted. The painter would have added the details of the armour to the basic shape created by the sculptor. Note the boss on the shield and compare it with the boss on the shield below.

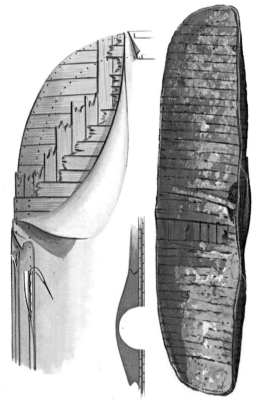

Above and *right:* This shield from Egypt has been identified as Celtic but is probably Roman. There is no other example of a curved Celtic shield but compare it with the sculpture on p. 34. This shield was made of laminated strips of wood covered with sheep's wool felt. There is a double row of stitching along the edge.

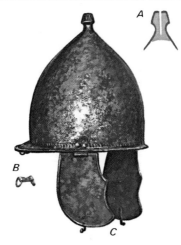

Types of helmet

Above: Montefortino type with a hole in the top for the crest pin. The top knot (A) was filled with lead to secure the pin. Under the peak at the back was a double ring (B) from which straps passed under the chin and fixed to the hooks on the cheek pieces (C).

Below: Helmet of Attic type with feather tubes.

Top: Etrusco-Corinthian helmet. This helmet was a corrupt form of the famous Greek face-covering helmet. It did not come down over the face but was worn like a cap on top of the head.

Above: The sculpture comes from a late Etruscan urn and shows an Etrusco-Corinthian helmet complete with crest and feathers.

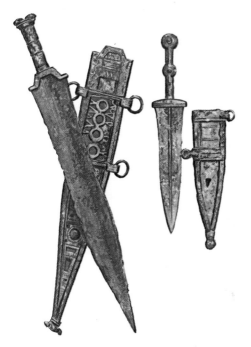

Above: A Spanish sword and dagger.

Below: Roman weapons from Numantia. Scale1:6.
1. Spear head.
2. Head of a light javelin of a veles.
3. Heavy pilum head.
4. Pilum head showing barbed point.
5. Light pilum head.
6. Reconstruction of a light veles javelin, a heavy pilum and a light pilum.

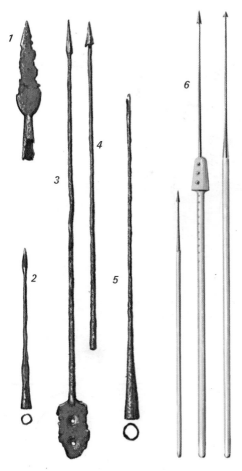

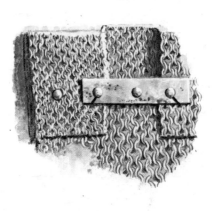

Above: A detail from a relief at Pergamum showing a Celtic mail shirt.

Right: Celtic mail from Romania (actual size). The iron rings were of two types: (A) punched out of a sheet and (B) wire which was butted (pushed) together after linking. These were used alternately.

The Navy: the Rise of Roman Sea Power

Right: A bas-relief of a war galley (late 1st century BC). It probably commemorates Augustus's victory over Antony and Cleopatra. If the decoration along the outrigger represents shipped oars, this could well be the flag ship of Augustus's navy with three banks of two-man oars.

After Pydna

After the Battle of Pydna Perseus fled to the island of Samothrace where he was captured by the Roman fleet. From there, he and his family were sent to Rome to grace the victor's Triumph.

The Navy during the Republic

Rome's rival, Carthage, had the largest fleet in the western Mediterranean. At the outbreak of the first Carthaginian war in 264 BC Rome found herself forced to compete. She built 100 ships based on a wrecked Carthaginian example.

The warship of the ancient Mediterranean was the galley: a boat rowed by more than one bank of oars. The standard warship of Rome was a five-banker (quinquereme). The normal method of sea fighting was for ships to try to ram each other with the beak that protruded from the front of the ship just below water level. This manoeuvre obviously required great skill.

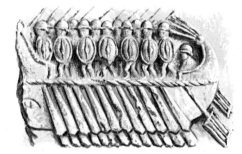

Above: A galley with two banks of oars (2nd–1st century BC)

The "Raven"

The Romans, however, were no seamen. They developed a boarding plank with a long spike at the end which swivelled on a pole mounted on the prow of the ship. The sailors nick-named this the "raven" (*corvus*) because of its beak.

The plank was dropped onto the deck of the enemy ship where the beak either stuck in the deck or hooked over the gunwales locking the two ships together. Rome had great success with this device and in the first battle captured 50 ships.

The Romans had continued success in sea battles, and built up a fleet of 350 ships. But although the ships were excellent fighting platforms, they were unseaworthy. Where the enemy failed the weather often succeeded. The fleet was caught in a storm off the coast of Sicily and 270 ships were wrecked with a loss of possibly 100,000 lives. Perhaps it was the *corvus* that made these ships so topheavy; whether this was so or not, we never hear of it again.

When the news of this staggering disaster reached Rome, the Senate ordered the rebuilding of the fleet. In three months, 200 new ships were launched. The Carthaginian navy was decisively defeated in 241 BC. From that day on, Rome never lost command of the sea.

The age of the sea battle was over. The only later engagement of any size was fought between Roman and Roman, i.e. between Augustus and Mark Antony at Actium in 31 BC.

Below: The front of a galley with three banks of oars (1st century BC).

The command

If the whole fleet was involved, the consul commanded. As on land, the omens were taken before the battle. During the first war with Carthage, one consul called for the augurs (seers) and was told that the sacred chickens would not eat. The consul was eager for battle and ordered the augurs to try again. When this was to no avail he grabbed the squawking birds and threw them into the sea with the famous last words "If the sacred chickens won't eat, let them drink". Naturally he was defeated.

The later years of the Republic

After the defeat of Carthage the Romans began to rely on the Greek states for ships and crews. The subsequent decline in naval strength allowed a rise in piracy. Pompey fought a campaign against the pirates and Caesar was actually captured by them. But after being ransomed he hunted them down.

Reconstruction of a Roman quinquereme from the 3rd century BC. This type of ship had a crew of 300 seamen and 120 marines. It was really a floating platform for infantry. The sail and mast are being lowered in preparation for battle.

The Navy of the Empire

After the defeat of Antony at Actium, Augustus was left with a fleet of about 700 ships. The ships were of all sizes and from them he selected the best to form a permanent Roman fleet. Although Antony had had some very large ships, Augustus wisely kept nothing larger than a six-banker, which became his own flagship.

Augustus based his two main fleets at Misenum in the Bay of Naples and at Ravenna at the mouth of the Po. He later added a further two—for Egypt and Syria. These fleets were used mainly to police the sea lanes. Later, for the conquest of Britain, a fleet was based at Boulogne in northern France. There were also fleets on the Rhine, Danube and Black Sea. These fleets were mainly used for the support and transport of land-troops.

Crews

The imperial fleets were commanded by prefects, individual ships by *trierarchs* (named after the captains of Greek triremes). The crew of a quinquereme was 300 seamen and 120 marines. There is no evidence whatsoever for slave labour in the galleys. All seamen were also soldiers and proud of it. The fleets were organized in much the same fashion as the auxiliaries (see page 54). Seamen served for 26 years and received a grant of Roman citizenship on discharge. Marines were commanded in the same fashion as legionaries.

Above: A marine from the imperial fleet at Misenum.

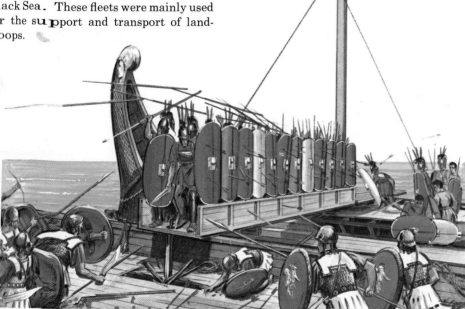

Above: The corvus in action. The soldiers go along the plank two abreast protected by their shields resting on the knee-high fence. In this way the Romans could use their superb infantry even at sea.

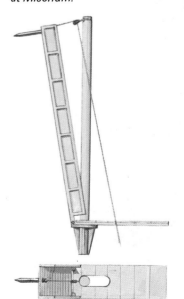

Right: The corvus was made in two sections 4 metres and 8 metres long. It was 1.2 metres wide and had a knee-high fence at either side. At the end was a long spike. The plank swivelled around a pole 8 metres high.

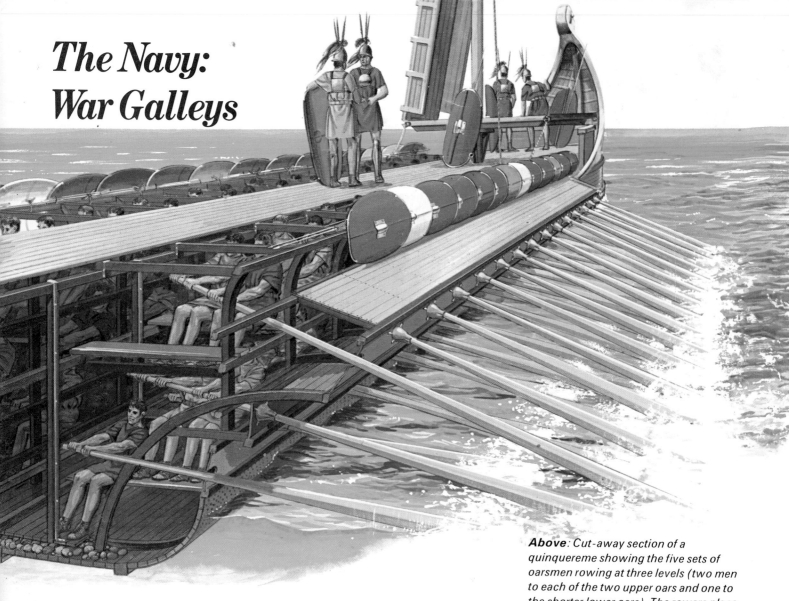

The Navy: War Galleys

Above: Cut-away section of a quinquereme showing the five sets of oarsmen rowing at three levels (two men to each of the two upper oars and one to the shorter lower oars). The rowers place their shields along the gunwales to protect themselves from missiles.

Above: A Roman anchor complete with wood frame, lead stock and rope. It was excavated at Lake Nemi from an imperial pleasure barge.

War galleys

The galley was developed by the Greeks and Phoenicians. Between 1000 and 400 BC they gradually increased the number of oars, producing ships with two (biremes), three (triremes), four (quadriremes) and five (quinqueremes) banks. The standard Roman warship was the quinquereme.

Although there is still some controversy over how the trireme was rowed, it is generally agreed that there was one man per oar and that the three banks were at different levels.

We know that the trireme had 170 oars with 62 rowers at the top level and 54 at each of the two lower levels. We also know from excavations of galley sheds in Greece that trireme and quinquereme sheds were much the same size—about 40 metres long and 5 metres wide. It therefore comes as some surprise to find that a set of oars for a quinquereme cost less than a set for a trireme. The only possible conclusion must be that a quinquereme had fewer oars.

Polybius tells us that quinqueremes had a crew of 300 seamen and 120 marines. Now the crew of a trireme was 200, of whom 170 were rowers. It should follow therefore, that on a quinquereme there should be about 260/270 rowers but fewer than 170 oars.

It would be very difficult to row a galley at more than four levels, as the oars would be too long to handle. According to Polybius, Perseus's flag ship had 16 *remes*. These bigger galleys then, were probably only developments of the trireme and were rowed at three levels; the number of *remes* therefore refers to the files of rowers.

Allowing up to seven men to an oar (this was the largest number used in 16th century galleys) up to 20 *remes* is possible at three levels.

If the quinquereme had two men per oar in the upper two banks where the boat was widest and one per oar below, we arrive at a boat with roughly 60 oars at the top level and 50 oars at the other two levels, with 270 rowers.

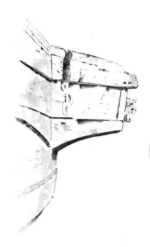

Left: Front view of the outrigger of a galley (from the full size sculpture of part of a galley on the Sacred Island in the Tiber).

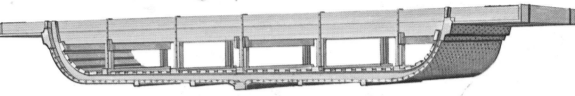

Left: The planks joined with mortices.

Below: Section of one of two imperial barges excavated from Lake Nemi. This huge galley was 70 metres long and 20 metres wide. The hull was completely sheathed in lead.

The outrigger

It was discovered early in the development of the galley that if the rowlocks could be extended beyond the side of the boat, greater leverage could be applied to the oar. An outrigger was therefore developed. This is the piece that juts out from the side of the galley at the level of the upper bank.

Sails and rudders

Oars were the main power source of the galley but if the wind was favourable a mast and square sail could be raised. Later galleys also had a small sprit sail at the front. These sails and mast would always be taken down before battle commenced. Ancient ships had no rudder but were steered by a pair of wide oars at the back.

Armament

Besides the underwater ram at the front of the ship and the "raven", galleys also carried catapults and other siege machines. During the siege of the port of Syracuse in the war with Hannibal, the Romans lashed two ships together and mounted a siege tower on them in order to attack the city walls from the sea. Battering rams are often depicted on ships and also towers such as that seen on the Praenestine ship (see page 20). These towers were primarily for raising archers and javelineers above the level of the other ship to enable them to rake the decks. These towers were made of wood and would be dismantled after the battle.

Construction

Roman and Greek ships were not constructed in the same way as mediaeval ones. The outside of the ship was built first and the frame inserted later.

The planks on the hull did not overlap as in Viking ships but were butted together and were held in place by mortices and dowels (see illustration above). The whole hull of a galley was sheathed in lead as is shown not only by the Nemi ship above, but also by the recent discovery of a Carthaginian wreck off the coast of Sicily.

Above: A sculpture from the museum at Sperlonga showing the housing of one of the steering oars. The stern rudder as we know it did not come into use until the end of the 12th century. Before that ships were steered by two large oars on either side of the stern.

This sculpture from the early Empire shows the handle of the steering oar projecting through the end of the outrigger.

Below: The front of a galley from Trajan's Column showing a ship from the Danube fleet. It has a sprit sail and a battering ram.

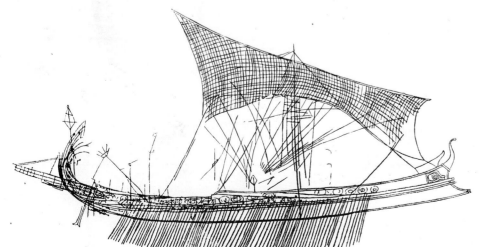

Left: A graffito from Delos of a galley of the 1st century BC. This shows a most complex rigging for control of sail and mast.

A scene from Caesar's great siege of Alesia. The relieving Gallic army has burst through the Roman defences. The legionaries, using their pila as spears, try to hold them at bay. Afterwards, when Caesar brought up his cavalry, the legionaries threw their pila and charged in with their swords.

The Army at the Time of Caesar

In the 50 years after the Battle of Pydna, Rome made few territorial gains. Her grip tightened on Spain, Tunisia and Greece and she conquered southern France to secure the land route to Spain. But little was done to extend her domain further.

Then, a series of military reforms at the end of the 2nd century BC produced a new type of army. It was composed of long-service soldiers loyal, not to the state, but to their generals. With the birth of this new-style army we enter the short but brilliant age of the adventurer generals.

Within the next 50 years, Rome doubled the size of her Empire. Her generals marched to the east and north. By the middle of the 1st century BC, Caesar had conquered Gaul and invaded Britain. Lucullus had crossed the Euphrates into southern Russia, and Pompey had stood in the Temple at Jerusalem. But with this new-style army the horrors of civil war were to come too, as general fought general.

During this period of Rome's growth, the central European tribes had periodically invaded Italy. On one occasion they had even sacked Rome. Although the legions had subsequently conquered those who had settled in Italy, the tribes beyond the Alps remained a constant threat. Around the time of Caesar's birth (100 BC) vast hordes of Germans had poured south and it was only after much bloodshed that the invasion of Italy was prevented.

Now, 40 years later, the tribes were once more on the move. Caesar seized this opportunity for obtaining wealth and glory and led his legions into central France. The background to the study of the army of this period will be Caesar's Gallic War. Our main source is Caesar's own account of his campaigns. Although this is not free from political propaganda, it is still a crucial source of information compiled by Rome's most successful soldier.

The New Legions

The problem of Gaul

The Romans believed that they could only hope to secure the safety of Italy by controlling the movement of the tribes of central Europe. The Rhone valley below Switzerland was brought under Roman control towards the end of the 2nd century BC. It became known as 'The Province' from which the French name for the area, Provence, is derived. It was from here that Caesar set about his conquest of the interior.

The people of Switzerland were called the Helvetii. They were dissatisfied with the harsh, barren lands

Above: The new long-service professional legionary. All legionaries were armed alike, with bronze helmet, mail shirt, oval shield, Spanish sword and light and heavy pila.

The citizen soldier

It had originally been the custom of the Roman state to place the defence of the fatherland only in the hands of the property-owning class who had some material interest in its survival.

The soldier was only called up when needed, and he was discharged as soon as the emergency was over. He was expected to provide his own armour. Although he was paid a small amount for his time in service, his main source of income was his farm or his business interests at home.

It is hardly surprising, therefore, that 'he was not keen on long periods of service. Consequently, recruiting became increasingly difficult as the theatre of war moved further from home and the periods of campaigning became longer. Those who were recruited were forever agitating for discharge.

The reforms of Marius

Towards the end of the 2nd century BC, Rome became involved in a long drawn-out war in Algeria. This war was so unattractive that it became almost impossible for Rome to find any recruits for her legions.

Marius was the Roman consul in charge of the war. Under these difficult circumstances, he threw the legions open to any volunteer who could claim Roman citizenship, regardless of whether he

owned property. The poor flocked to join the legions. Far from seeking an early discharge from the army, they hoped that their service would continue indefinitely. The foundations of a professional army were laid.

Permanent legions

Under the old system the legions were re-enrolled for every campaign and could never gain a lasting sense of identity. This was all changed. Soon after Marius's reforms, legions were formed that continued to exist throughout the life of the Empire.

Pay and equipment

In the past, recruits had been very poorly paid, yet they had still been expected to supply their own armour. The new legionaries were poor and could not possibly afford to supply their own armour so their pay was raised to cover this cost. The number of cheap mass-produced helmets that come from this period illustrate the dramatic change in the composition of the legions.

As all legionaries could now afford to be fully armed the distinction between heavy and light armed troops was abolished. The *velites* of the time of Aemilius Paullus, who had been lightly-armed with only javelins and shields, disappeared from history.

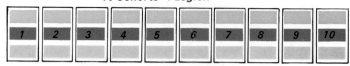

1 Cohort

Triarii
Principes
Hastati

10 Cohorts = 1 Legion

| 1 | 2 | 3 | 4 | 5 | 6 | 7 | 8 | 9 | 10 |

The re-organized legion. The maniples of triarii, hastati and principes were joined to form ten cohorts.

along the foot of the Alps, and were planning to move out and settle in France. In spite of Roman threats, a vast host of men, women and children—over a third of a million of them—moved into France. Caesar marched north to turn them back. In the battle that followed, the carnage was so great that the very name of the Helvetii was almost eliminated from history.

However, it was not only the Helvetii who posed a threat to peace in France. The Germans had been crossing the Rhine and had settled on its western banks. Caesar now ordered them to withdraw and when they refused he forced them to battle and drove them back across the river. Although Caesar may not have planned it, he now realized that only by permanently occupying Gaul could the Romans hope to maintain a tribal balance in the area. With this in mind, he set about the conquest of the tribes around the borders.

First he marched into Belgium, crushing all before him. He was already preoccupied with the idea of an expedition to Britain and so he also had to bring the maritime tribes of the coast under his control. Splitting his army, he set about the conquest of northern and western France.

Below: A military tribune. These young aristocratic officers held their posts to further their political careers. The generals of this era were embarrassed by the tribunes' lack of experience and placed command of the legions in the hands of a legatus, an older man with more experience.

The helmet and cuirass on the left are a general's and those on the right possibly a centurion's. They come from a triumphal monument dating from the late Republic.

Reorganization

It was at about this time that a fundamental rethinking about the shape of the legion took place.

The maniples of *triarii* were raised to the same strength as the *hastati* and *principes* and coupled with them to form cohorts. Thus the whole legion now consisted of ten cohorts instead of 30 maniples.

The distinction between the *hastati/principes* and the *triarii* was also dropped now, and all were armed alike with sword and *pilum*.

A few years later, all Italians living south of the river Po were granted Roman citizenship. This meant that the distinction between Roman and allied legions was abolished. From this point one legion means exactly what it says and does not imply an equal number of soldiers from the cities allied to Rome.

Marius's mules

On the march the old army had always been accompanied by a large baggage train. These baggage trains not only offered a great temptation to the enemy but also slowed down the army. Marius made the legionary carry his essential supplies on his back and because of this legionaries became known as Marius's mules.

The Legion command

The legion was still commanded by six tribunes. By Caesar's time, however, these were generally young aristocrats who were merely putting in the necessary military service to qualify for a magistracy. They were therefore men of little or no experience. The generals of this period overcame this weakness by placing legions under the overall command of a *legatus*.

Military Engineering: Bridges

During Caesar's campaigns along the northern coast of Europe, the Germans crossed the Rhine again. Caesar turned south and massacred them without mercy, driving the survivors back across the river. Then he decided that he would over-awe these tribes with a display of Roman engineering skill.

The fast flowing Rhine was the largest and most powerful river that the Romans had ever seen. It was seldom less than half a kilometre in width. The crossing had to be made by boats, and it was assumed that it would be impossible to bridge the river.

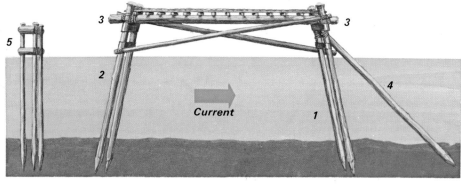

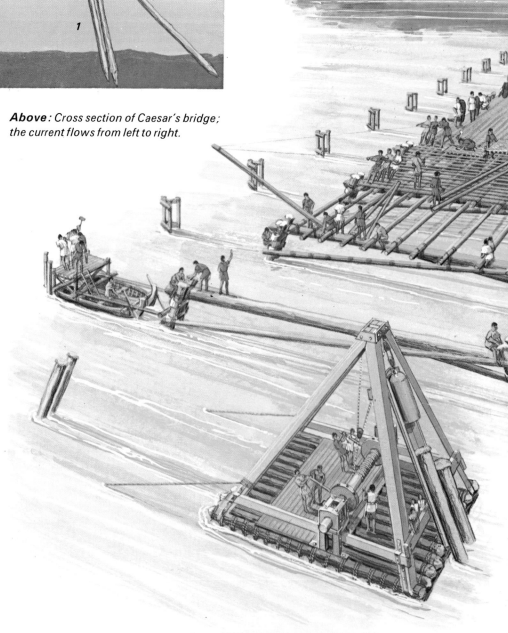

Above: Cross section of Caesar's bridge; the current flows from left to right.

Bridge builders

Rome itself was built at the only bridge-able spot on the lower Tiber and hence controlled all the traffic passing from Tuscany to southern Italy. The Romans excelled at bridge building and their high priest assumed, as the Pope does today, the title of Bridge-Builder-in-Chief (*Pontifex Maximus*). In 62 BC, the rebuilding of the Bridge of Fabricius across the Tiber was ordered. The Senate refused to pay for it until its durability had been tested. More than 2000 years later, heavy traffic still trundles across this bridge.

Military bridges

The army used three types of bridge. If the current was not too strong, a series of boats was lashed together and a roadway placed across them.

Caesar needed something stronger to cross the Rhine, so he built a series of wooden trestles to support his roadway. He probably crossed at Coblenz, where the Rhine is about half a kilometre wide and up to 8 metres deep.

At the beginning of the 2nd century AD, the Emperor Trajan invaded Dacia and built Rome's finest military bridge, across the Danube at the Iron Gates. It was 1500 metres long and was built on 20 massive stone piers 50 metres high and 20 metres wide.

Nevertheless, Caesar constructed a bridge in the short space of ten days and led his army across. The Germans fled before him in astonishment. But this tremendous feat served only as a propaganda exercise. Eighteen days later, Caesar withdrew and destroyed his bridge behind him.

After his expedition into Germany Caesar set about his projected invasion of Britain. He and his army sailed across the channel twice in two successive years, but his plan seemed to be mainly to impress; not the local British tribes as he had done in Germany, but the Senate at Rome. As in Germany,

he withdrew completely.

The tribes of central France had welcomed the Romans as friends at first. They now began to realize that Caesar had no intention of leaving and that they were having to support his vast army. In the winter of 54-53 BC the Gallic tribes of the north-east rose and attacked the Romans in their winter camps. One and a half legions were massacred, but the revolt was only partial and inevitably ended in defeat for the Gauls. The following spring Caesar held court and executed or outlawed several of the Gallic chiefs for their part in the uprising.

Above: Bridge of boats from Trajan's Column.

Above: Trajan's bridge across the Danube, also from Trajan's Column. The superstructure of this bridge was of wood supported on 20 massive stone piles.

Below: The Roman bridge at Alcantara in Spain. This bridge, dating from the time of Trajan, was built in much the same way as Trajan's Danube bridge, but the superstructure was of stone. This bridge is still in use today.

Caesar's bridge across the Rhine. A pair of timbers (1) was rammed into the river bed, inclining against the current. Twelve metres upstream a second pair (2) was rammed in inclining downstream. These were joined by a cross beam (3). A series of trestles made like this supported the road. The trestles were further supported by a timber slanting against the current (4). A short distance upstream, breakwaters (5) were set up to prevent anything being carried against the trestles.

Military Engineering: Roads and Ramps

Gallic tribes rise again under Vercingetorix

Caesar had now shown that he regarded the Gauls as a conquered people, not as allies. In the spring of 52 BC the tribes rose again in a concerted effort under the command of Vercingetorix, a skilled leader. Caesar raced back from Italy to take command.

The Gauls had planned a scorched earth policy and withdrew before him burning towns and crops. The people of Avaricum believed their town to be impregnable and refused to abandon it. Within a month Caesar's veterans had stormed the town and slain every living thing in it.

Above: Section of a typical Roman road. It was 5-6 metres wide with a drainage ditch on each side. The four levels were of sand, slabs of stone in cement, crushed stone in cement, and stone blocks.

Left: Traces of the Roman road over the Great St Bernard Pass.

Snow-covered alpine passes

Polybius tells us that all the alpine passes were snow-covered all the year round and modern investigation has shown this to be true. Caesar did not succeed in opening the Great St Bernard but his nephew, Augustus, did. The ancient geographer Strabo described it as "a precipitous short cut where no wheeled vehicle could pass". Traces of the road still survive.

The network of roads

The great military roads are the most enduring relic of Rome's power. A vast network has been found stretching all over Europe. In many places the old road is still used and in many more the road of today follows the course of the ancient military highway.

The army constructed roads into newly conquered territories from the earliest times. Fortified towns (colonies; see page 56) were established at strategic points. The roads connected these strongholds to enable the legions to move quickly to their support.

It was this extensive system of roads and strongholds that enabled the Romans to hold out against Hannibal in their darkest hour.

No obstacle too great

There was nowhere that the Roman roads did not go; no obstacle seemed to be too great. We find roads across marshes, through tunnels and over mountains. Even today you can still see where the road has been hewn out of the cliff face along the Danube by the military engineers of Trajan's day.

The route to central France was a long winding road. It passed through the Alps and emerged in the Rhone valley about 130 kilometres south of Lyons. The Romans soon needed a shorter route. Early in his Gallic campaigns we read of Caesar contemplating opening the pass over the Great St Bernard. In those days it was more than 500 metres above the level of the permanent snow.

A soldier's job

Although the army did much road building it is obvious that the soldiers hated the work and letters have been found from soldiers grumbling about it.

A letter from one soldier in the east tells of how he has been sent to assist some civilians who are having difficulties building an aqueduct. The soldier comments "If you want a decent job done, get the army to do it". Arriving at the scene of the building, the legionary discovers that the difficulties have arisen when the "civilians" were boring a tunnel through a hill. The tunnel had been started from both sides. "I took measurements of both tunnels," the soldier remarks wryly, "and found that the sum of the two measurements was greater than the width of the hill"!

Vercingetorix continued his retreat and took up his position on the hill fort of Gergovia. The legions attempted to storm the hill but overstretched themselves. For the first time Caesar suffered a reverse in the field. He himself admits that he lost 700 men and no less than 46 centurions.

The Gallic spirits rose. Their cavalry launched a surprise attack on the legions, but Caesar's newly-recruited German cavalry saved them from disaster. The Gallic horsemen were routed. Vercingetorix retired hastily to Alesia, another hill fort, and prepared to withstand a siege.

Siege tactics: ramps

Although the Romans' engineering feats make us gaze with wonder, it was in their siege works that they really excelled. Their mastery stemmed mainly from a combination of skill, discipline, energy and sheer doggedness.

The Romans had two types of siege tactic. The first was to build ramps and towers against the enemy walls in order to storm a town. The second was to erect defensive walls around the town in order to cut it off and starve the inhabitants out.

The soldiers preferred the first as the booty would be theirs; the commander preferred the second for then it would be his. Caesar gives us a vivid description of both types: the assault at Avaricum described on this page and the blockade at Alesia (see page 32).

The Siege of Avaricum

The town of Avaricum was situated on a spur of high ground jutting out into the marshes. The spur first slopes down and then rises to a small hillock at its end. The town itself was on this hillock. Caesar's troops attacked along the spur. Within a month they had built a massive mound to fill in the depression and had then raised it to the level of the top of the town wall. Now the legionaries could storm the town.

This was typical of the Roman method of storming and was used in both Roman sieges of Jerusalem. The vast amount of timber required for these works provoked the Jewish historian Josephus to remark that during the siege of Jerusalem not a tree was left standing within 18 kilometres.

Below: Caesar's siege works at Avaricum. In order to storm the town, Caesar filled the dip between his camp and the town with a massive ramp 100 metres broad and 25 metres high. Along this he moved his siege towers and brought his men up to the walls through galleries.

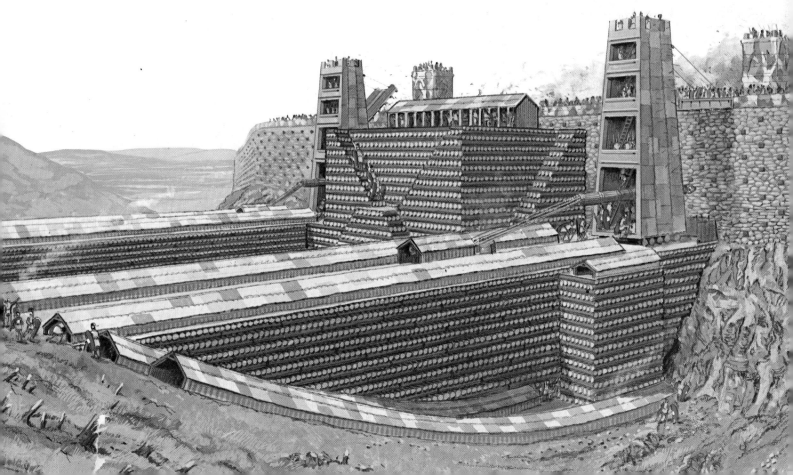

Blockades

The siege of Alesia

Vercingetorix sent his cavalry from Alesia to raise a fresh army and then prepared to withstand a siege. Caesar raised two lines of fortifications around the town and encamped between them.

Food soon ran short in the town. In desperation Vercingetorix turned out all those who could not fight—old men, women and children. They begged Caesar to accept them into slavery but he refused to let them through his lines. Rejected by friend and foe, they starved to death between the lines.

The relieving force was estimated at a quarter of a

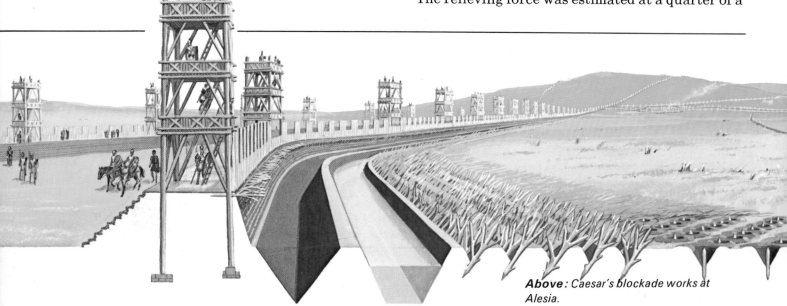

Above: Caesar's blockade works at Alesia.

The Siege of Alesia

Alesia was situated on a lozenge-shaped plateau, 1500 metres long, 1000 metres wide and 150 metres high. On three sides were valleys, beyond which hills rose steeply. On the western side was a small plain. Streams flowed to the north and south of the hill. The town itself covered only the western part of the plateau. Vercingetorix's army of 80,000 men occupied the other half.

Caesar decided upon a blockade. He encamped his legions on the hills around the town and traced out the line of his siege works. Along this line he constructed 23 forts. He then set his soldiers to work digging the trenches.

First they dug a vertical trench six metres wide right across the plain at the foot of the plateau. This prevented any attack on his men as they were erecting the main works. 400 metres behind this trench they dug two ditches five metres wide. Where possible, they filled the inner one with water. These two ditches were extended all the way along the foot of the hills that surrounded the town until they formed a complete circuit 16 kilometres long.

The rampart

The earth from these ditches was piled up beyond the outer trench to form a rampart. Along the top of this the Romans set up a palisade with towers every 25 metres. Pointed stakes were embedded in the top of the rampart, and projected horizontally.

Many of Caesar's men were away collecting timber and food, so the number of troops guarding the palisade had to be greatly reduced. Caesar dug five more trenches 1.5 metres deep to compensate for this. He set pointed branches in them to form a hedge of spikes.

In front of this hedge of spikes Caesar dug eight rows of circular pits into which he stuck sharpened stakes. The troops called them lilies because of their similarity to the flowers. He then covered these with brushwood to hide them from the attackers. Similar pits to these have been found in front of the Antonine Wall in Scotland.

Beyond the pits he planted small logs about 30 centimetres long with barbed spikes stuck in them. These were buried so that only the top of the spike protruded from the ground.

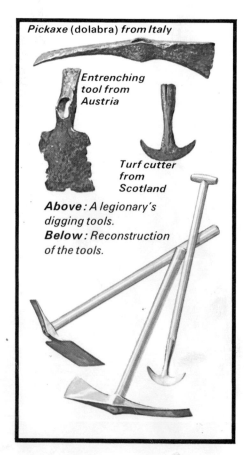

Pickaxe (dolabra) from Italy

Entrenching tool from Austria

Turf cutter from Scotland

Above: A legionary's digging tools.
Below: Reconstruction of the tools.

million men. When they arrived, Caesar split his forces to guard the inner and outer defences. The Gauls threw themselves against the ramparts and were driven back again and again.

Two of the legions were encamped together on a hillside to the north of the town. The Gauls realized the weakness of this position and moved 60,000 of their troops round the back of the hill at night. The following day they launched an attack from above the camp. The remainder of the relieving force again charged the defences in the plain and Vercingetorix attacked from the inside.

The Gauls attacking the camp on the hillside filled the trenches and poured over the rampart. The legionaries used their *pila* as spears to hold them at bay. Meanwhile Caesar had managed to repulse Vercingetorix's attack. Calling his cavalry together, he rushed towards the beleaguered camp. The Roman soldiers saw his scarlet cloak as he rode across the plain, threw their *pila* into the mass of the enemy and charged with their swords. Caught between the legionaries and the cavalry, the Gauls were slaughtered. The following day Vercingetorix saw that all was lost and surrendered.

The outer lines
Caesar then built a similar set of defences facing outwards to keep out the relieving force. These outer lines stretched for over 20 kilometres and were similarly booby-trapped.

The siege works around Alesia were not unique. This method had been used to reduce Capua in the war with Hannibal. It had been used to reduce Numantia and had been used against Carthage herself when the city was destroyed.

The energy of the legionary
The energy of the legionary seemed boundless. When Paullus camped before Perseus at Pydna the legionaries cut 13,000 square metres of turf and lifted more than 20,000 cubic metres of earth in order to construct the ramparts.

Tools
This daily camp-constructing would have been completed in a couple of hours. The work would have been done entirely with the three main tools that the legionary carried: his pickaxe (*dolabra*); his turf cutter and his entrenching tool (which was very similar to that used by the British Army in World War I).

Prestige
The prestige and confidence of the Romans in siege works was enormous. A Roman commander was once informed by an envoy of a town that he was about to besiege that they had enough food for ten years. He replied casually that he would take it in the eleventh year. The result of this remark was that the town capitulated immediately.

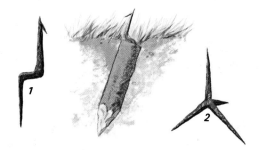

Above: **1.** An iron spike from Alesia. These were hammered into short logs and buried in the ground. **2.** A caltrop from Britain. These were used for the same purpose.

Below: The blockade lines around Alesia. The assaults of the relieving army and Vercingetorix are marked in orange.

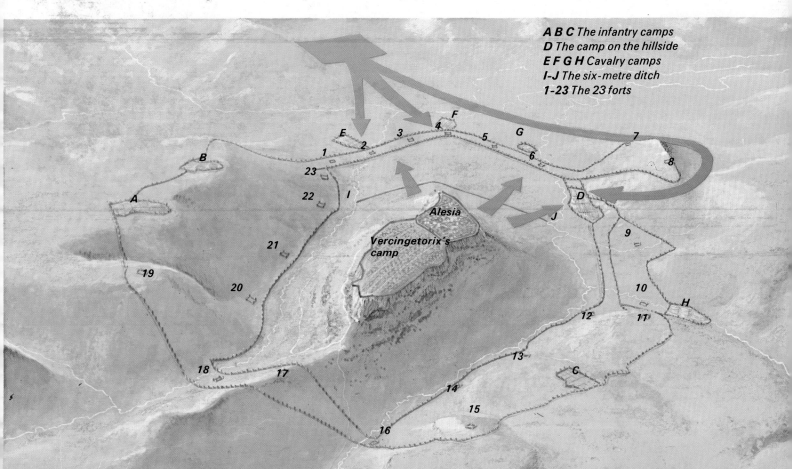

A B C The infantry camps
D The camp on the hillside
E F G H Cavalry camps
I-J The six-metre ditch
1-23 The 23 forts

Armour and Weapons of Caesar's Time

Evidence from sculpture

There is unfortunately very little evidence for the arms and armour of the 1st century BC. There is only one military sculpture that shows legionaries. This sculpture is known as the Altar of Domitius Ahenobarbus and illustrates a group of soldiers, possibly being discharged from service.

The group comprises four legionaries and an officer, probably a tribune. The four legionaries all wear coats of mail and all carry the large oval *scutum*, as on the relief at Delphi (see page 18).

Armour

One legionary wears a Montefortino type helmet and the other three Etrusco-Corinthian types. All have long horse-hair crests hanging from their helmets but no feathers. None of the legionaries wear greaves on their legs.

Although no archaeological examples of body armour for this period exist, we do have several helmets of different types.

The officer wears a short muscled cuirass, a Greek type of armour adopted by the officer class in Italy. There are several examples of this type of cuirass in existence.

The officer wears a heavy tunic under his cuirass, with two overlapping skirts of *pteriges*. These were broad protective strips which were usually of leather. This tunic has similar strips at the shoulders and is worn over his normal tunic.

He also wears greaves and an Etrusco-Corinthian type helmet with horse-hair crest. Behind him stands a large round shield. Around his waist he wears a sash which is knotted at the front with the loose ends tucked up at either side—the symbol of his high rank.

Above: *A montage of soldiers from the Altar of Domitius Ahenobarbus. Note the mail shirts. The soldier on the right has mail extending over the shoulders; he also has a clearly marked boss on his shield.*

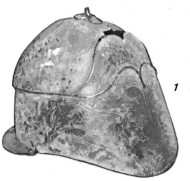

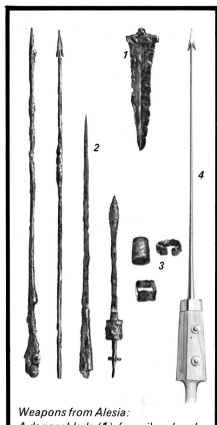

Weapons from Alesia:
A dagger blade (1), four pilum *heads (2) with both square and round ferrules (3), a reconstructed heavy* pilum *(4).*

The late Republican helmets:
1. An Etrusco-Corinthian type. The eye-holes have disappeared but are still faintly marked.
2. A typical poor quality mass-produced Montefortino helmet.
3. A late Hellenistic helmet of the type worn by officers.

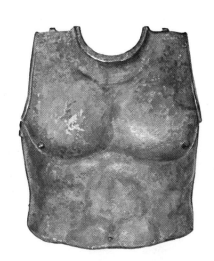

Above: *An officer from the Altar of Domitius Ahenobarbus. He wears a short muscled cuirass and a helmet of either type (1) or (3) above. He also wears greaves and carries a spear and round shield. Around his waist he wears a sash, the symbol of his rank.*

Left: *The front plate of a Greek-type short muscled cuirass. This sort of cuirass was worn by officers in the Roman army from the Republic right through into the Empire.*

Weapons

French excavations took place in the 1860's at the site of Caesar's great siege at Alesia. These produced a wealth of assorted weapons, among which are a dagger and several *pilum* heads. Unfortunately no Roman sword has been recovered. It is almost certain that the blade was slightly waisted and had a long point, for this type was still in use early in the Empire (see page 51).

We know that at the time of Marius the *pilum* head was held to the wooden shaft by two rivets and therefore was of the flat tanged type, similar to the heavy *pilum* from Numantia. There is a very corroded specimen from Alesia which may be identified with this type. Marius found that the long iron shaft of this type of *pilum* was not always bending on impact and that it was being thrown back by the enemy. He therefore removed one rivet and replaced it with a wooden dowel which splintered on impact.

Caesar overcame this same problem by leaving the metal below the point untempered. There are also examples of the socketed type of light *pila* from Alesia.

35

The Army of the Empire

The Army of the Empire will be described against the background of events that occurred at the end of Nero's reign. At this time the armies revolted against the Emperor and tried to put their own commanders on the throne. We shall also deal with the Jewish revolt.

Our main sources are: Tacitus, who grew up during the reign of Nero; Josephus, a Jew who turned traitor to his own people during the Jewish revolt, and Vegetius, who wrote a manual of military oddments towards the end of the 4th century AD.

Tacitus is our most reliable source. He wrote a history of the 1st century AD and also a book on Germany of the same period. He was the son-in-law of the great Agricola who was Governor of Britain for seven years and completed the conquest of that country.

Josephus, who wrote a history of the Jewish revolt, is not a reliable source. He exaggerates greatly, especially when describing his own exploits against the Romans before he changed sides. However, he does have some useful information and gives a very powerful account of the fall of Jerusalem.

Vegetius is an historian with a fly-paper mind. He offers a mass of unrelated facts collected from all periods of Roman history. He can only be used to supply details.

To these sources we must also add Trajan's Column with its great spiral relief which records the campaigns of the Emperor Trajan at the beginning of the 2nd century AD.

Legionaries are caught off guard and attacked while they are building siege ramps against the fortress of Antonia in Jerusalem. Roman siege towers with battering rams are being moved up to the walls whilst catapults bombard the battlements.

The Frontiers

1 Legion *II Augusta* at Gloucester
2 Legion *IX Hispana* at Lincoln
3 Legion *XX Valeria Victrix* near Shrewsbury
4 Legions *V Alaudae* and *XV Primigenia* at Xanten
5 Legion *XVI Gallica* at Neuss
6 Legion *I Germanica* at Bonn
7 Legions *IV Macedonica* and *XXII Primigenia* at Mainz
8 Legion *XXI Rapax* at Windisch
9 Legion *X Gemina* near Bratislava
10 Legion *XIII Gemina* near Budapest
11-14 Legions *XI Claudia, VIII Augusta, III Gallica* and *VII Claudia*
15 Legions *IV Scythica, XII Fulminata* and *VI Ferrata* near Antioch in Syria
16 Legions *V Macedonica, X Fretensis* and *XV Apollinaris* in Judaea
17 Legions *III Cyrenaica* and *XXII Deiotariana* at Alexandria
18 Legion *III Augusta* near border between Tunisia and Algeria
19 Legion *VI Victrix* in Spain
20 Legion *I Italica* in Italy
21 Legion *XIV Gemina* at Lyons

The distribution of the 28 legions in AD 68

The frontiers

After the conquest of Gaul, Rome was involved in 20 years of civil war. Supreme power fell into the hands of one man, Augustus, the nephew of Caesar. At the end of the civil war there were some 60 legions. Augustus reduced this number to 28.

Three legions were subsequently lost in an ambush in the forests of Germany, but by the end of Nero's reign, a hundred years later, the number had again been raised to 28. Twenty-five of these were garrisoned along the borders of the Empire. In the east, five legions were garrisoned near Antioch in Syria and three more were stationed in Egypt. Of these eight eastern legions, two Syrian and one Egyptian were on active service in Judaea putting down the Jewish revolt. There was only one more legion in the rest of North Africa.

No one doubted that one day the Empire would extend to the Baltic, but the northern advance of the legions had stopped at the natural frontiers of the Rhine and the Danube. Thirteen legions were encamped along this frontier poised to invade north-eastern Europe. Of the remaining six legions, three were stationed in Britain and one each in Spain, Gaul and Italy.

Besides these forces there were a similar number of soldiers drawn from the population along the frontiers. These were known as auxiliaries.

Permanent camps

The legions had built permanent camps at strategic points along the Rhine and Danube. These were similar to marching camps but had far stronger defences and the tents were replaced first with timber and later with stone buildings.

Along the Rhine, camps were already being built of stone by Nero's time. The British camps, being established much later, were not stone-built until around the end of the 1st century AD. The re-building of camps in stone took place probably when the timber camps were no longer serviceable.

The permanent camps were like small towns, completely self-sufficient with hospitals, workshops, schools etc.

The barrack blocks were built to hold a complete century each. The soldiers' accommodation was composed of ten or eleven sets of double rooms at one end of the building. Each double room consisted of a large bedroom about 4.5 metres square to hold eight legionaries, and a smaller room for their equipment. At the other end of the block were the century offices and the centurions' living quarters.

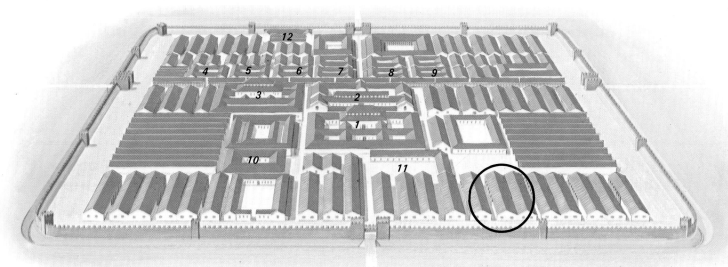

Layout of the camp

The barrack blocks were grouped in pairs facing each other in a way which echoes the manipular system of the Republic. They formed the perimeter of the built-up area of the camp: they were built about 30 metres back from the rampart to be out of range of missiles.

The camp was divided down the middle by the *via praetoria* which led straight to the administrative centre (*principia*) and the legion commander's house (*praetorium*) in the middle of the camp. Behind these was the main lateral road (*via principalis*), and beyond this, facing the road, were the tribunes' houses.

Above: The fortress of Legion XVI at Novaesium (Neuss) on the lower Rhine. It covers an area of 450×650 metres.
1. The commander's house (praetorium).
2. Legion headquarters (principia).
3. Hospital.
4–9. Tribunes' houses.
10. Workshops.
11. Market place.
12. Granaries and cookhouse.

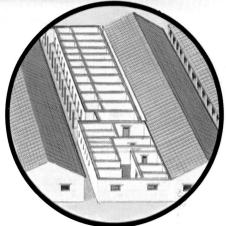

Above: The inset shows a century barrack block with double rooms for legionaries at the far end, and the centurions' quarters at the front.

Left: The principia *and behind it the* praetorium.

Defences of timber-built camps

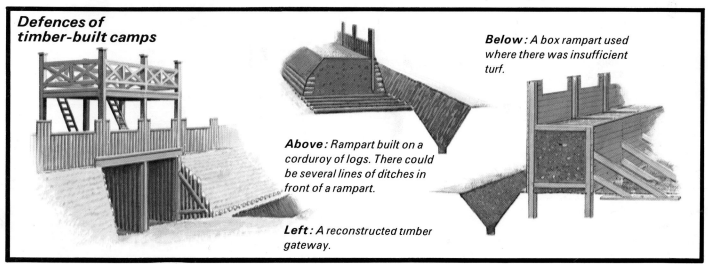

Above: Rampart built on a corduroy of logs. There could be several lines of ditches in front of a rampart.

Below: A box rampart used where there was insufficient turf.

Left: A reconstructed timber gateway.

The Legions of the Empire

Vindex rebels against Nero

By AD 68, the government of the Roman world had been in the hands of Nero for 14 years. Although he was loved in his early reign he had by now withdrawn into a world of his own, peopled only by his servile admirers. His companions encouraged his follies, and Nero spent his days reciting poetry, acting and playing the lyre. He no longer took any notice of the world's problems. During a severe shortage of food in the city, for example, vital ships were used to bring sand for the Emperor's stage.

Many plots were hatched against his life and many

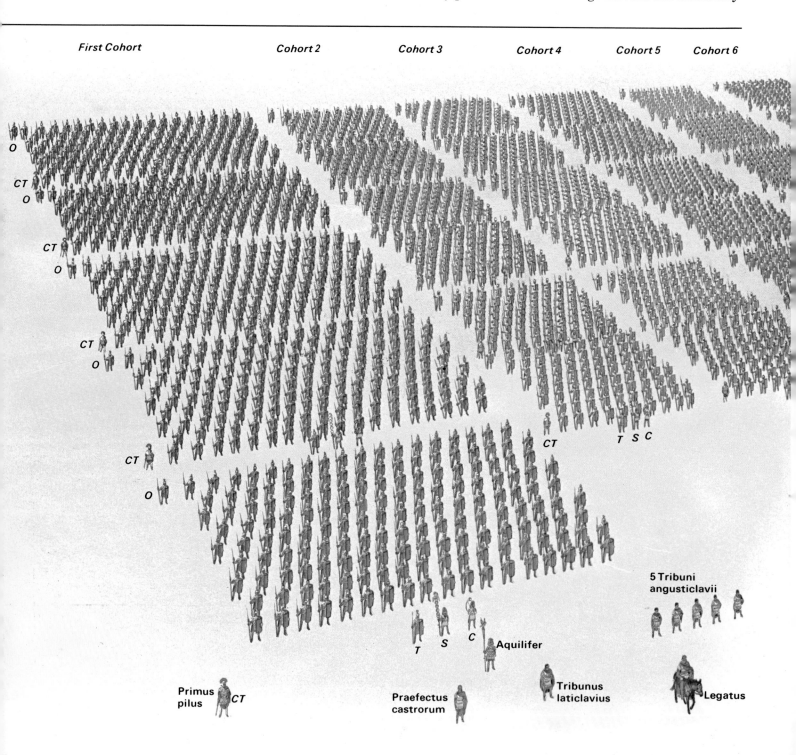

First Cohort   Cohort 2   Cohort 3   Cohort 4   Cohort 5   Cohort 6

O
CT
O
CT
O
CT
O
CT
O
CT
O

CT   T S C

5 Tribuni angusticlavii

T   S   C   Aquilifer

Primus pilus   CT

Praefectus castrorum

Tribunus laticlavius

Legatus

a noble head rolled. Nero trusted nobody. When the Jews revolted Nero sent Vespasian to put down the rebellion—but only as long as he could keep the general's younger son Domitian in Rome as a hostage for his father's loyalty. Little did the Emperor realize that within three years Vespasian would be sitting on his throne; and that three others would have sat there before him.

Nero felt that Greece alone could satisfy his artistic soul and he fled to that country. There he declared himself winner of the Olympic Games and returned to Rome with more than 1800 prizes. Mean-while, Vindex, the governor of central France, had become disgusted with Nero's antics. He wrote a letter to Galba, the governor of Spain, suggesting that Galba should take over the reins of government. He complained not only that Nero was unfit to rule but also that he was a terrible musician. Vindex's appeal opened a new era in Roman history. The legions now made the throne their own concern.

At first the plot to overthrow Nero failed as others had done before. The army of northern Germany marched into France and put Vindex and his hastily-gathered army to the sword.

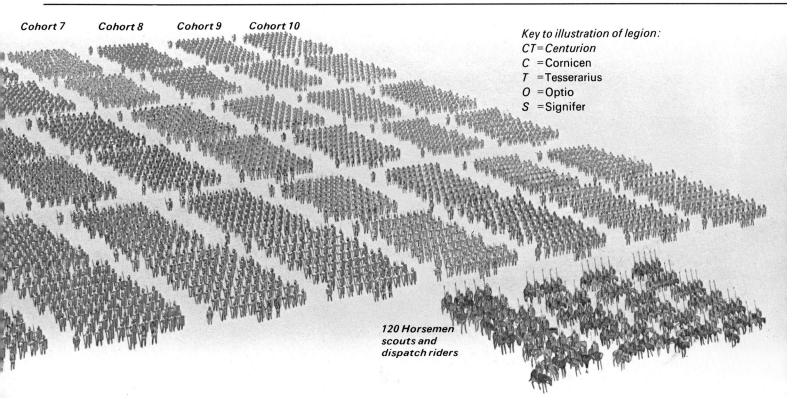

Cohort 7   Cohort 8   Cohort 9   Cohort 10

Key to illustration of legion:
CT = Centurion
C = Cornicen
T = Tesserarius
O = Optio
S = Signifer

120 Horsemen scouts and dispatch riders

The legions of the Empire

The legion of the early Empire was not very different from that of Caesar's time. Cohorts 2 to 10 still contained around 500 men each, organized into six centuries of about 80 men.

However, at some time in the second half of the 1st century AD the first cohort was expanded to about 800 men and reorganized into five instead of six centuries. Attached to the legion were 120 horsemen who acted as scouts and dispatch riders. This brought the man-power of the legion up to about 5,500.

There were 28 of these legions which were the cream of the army. Their job was primarily offensive and they would only really be brought into the field for further conquest, to put down a revolt or repel an invasion. Defence was left to the auxiliary regiments stationed in the frontier zone.

Recruitment

As in the previous periods, the legions continued to be recruited exclusively from Roman citizens. Citizenship had been granted to all Italians at the end of the Republic. In the same way, the cities of the provinces were gradually admitted to the rights of citizenship under the Empire. Thus we find that St Paul, who was a Jew from Turkey, can claim "I am a Roman citizen", in the middle of the 1st century AD.

The auxiliaries received Roman citizen-ship on discharge from service, so their sons could and often did become legion-aries.

The result of this gradual extension of citizenship was a progressive reduction in the numbers of Italians to be found serving in the army. Nevertheless, when a new legion was raised it still had to be recruited in Italy despite these changes.

Above: A late 1st century AD legion on parade. The legion strength at this time was about 5,500 men divided into ten cohorts. The first cohort was about 800 strong and the other cohorts about 500 strong.

Numbers of the legions

Many of the legions originated in the conflicting armies of the 20 years of civil war that raged between 50 and 30 BC. It was probably for this reason that some legionary numbers were duplicated (there were actually three third legions). When a legion was destroyed or dis-banded the number was never used again. The three Augustan legions XVII, XVIII and XIX which were destroyed in Germany in AD 9 were never replaced.

Praetorian and Urban Cohorts

The rise and fall of Galba

Vindex's revolt had repercussions. Now the army of northern Germany offered the title of Emperor to its own commander, Verginius. He declined the honour. If he had accepted, the course of history might have been changed. His refusal set off a chain of events that was to bring both Rome and her army to the depths of degradation.

The news of events on the Rhine reached Rome in a few days. It was not long before the Praetorian Guard showed interest. Their commander suggested that a new emperor might be very grateful if they raised

Above: *Standard of the 3rd Praetorian cohort with images of Nero and his wife.*

The Praetorian Guard

From earliest times a consul had twelve *lictors* who acted as his personal bodyguard. These men carried bundles of rods and axes as a symbol of the consul's power of life and death over the citizens. However it was found that these twelve men were not a sufficient bodyguard for the general while on active service. So it had become the job of the *extraordinarii* (see page 11) to act as guards to the consul.

Thirty years after the Battle of Pydna we find Scipio Aemilianus forming a personal bodyguard of 500 men, during the siege of Numantia. These became known as the Praetorian Guard, after the *praetorium*, the area of the camp where the general's tent was pitched. By the end of the Republic, all generals had a Praetorian cohort.

The Imperial Bodyguard

The Emperor Augustus formed these Praetorians into a special bodyguard for himself. He increased their number to nine cohorts (4,500 men), of which three were billeted in the city under his direct command. The others were stationed in towns around Rome. In 2 BC he gave them two commanders of their own, *praefecti praetorio*. Within 25 years, however, the command had become united under one man and the whole Guard had been brought into the city.

A new power

A very dangerous situation had come into being, for the true power lay not with the Emperor but with the commander of the Guard. In spite of this, the number of cohorts was raised to twelve (about 6,000 men), a short time later.

This power was used in AD 68 when the Guard was bribed to disown Nero. Later Otho used the same men to dispose of Galba. After the defeat of Otho, Vitellius

Above left: *Two* lictors *from the Cancelleria relief at Rome.*
Above right: *Praetorian guardsmen carrying traditional Republican shields from the same relief.*
Right: *A Praetorian in dress uniform and in battle dress.*

disbanded the Praetorian Guard and formed his own guard from the German legions, raising its number to 16,000, the equivalent of three legions.

Vespasian reinstated the original guard but reduced them to nine cohorts again. Domitian, the second son of Vespasian, raised the number once more to ten; this remained their strength until they were finally disbanded by Constantine in AD 312.

him to the throne. The commander then offered his men a large sum of money in the name of Galba. Their greed outweighed their loyalty and they dissolved their oath of allegiance to the Emperor. The Senate quickly followed suit and declared Nero a public enemy. The throne was offered to Galba and he accepted. Nero was now deserted by his guard and hated by his subjects. For all his Olympic "golds", he could do nothing. He tried to flee with one faithful slave but, finding escape cut off, he decided to die like a Roman. With a dagger clutched in his trembling hands the last of Caesar's descendants put an end to his miserable existence.

But the disease had not run its course. Otho had been a favourite at Nero's court until the Emperor had confiscated his wife. He had reason to hope that Galba, who was in his 70's, might name him as his successor. When this did not happen Otho approached the Praetorian Guard. They had not received their bribe and, once again, dissolved their oath of allegiance. Tearing Galba's image from their standards the Praetorians rushed to the Forum. Here they found the Emperor and brutally murdered him. Galba had ruled for only four months.

Pay and uniform

At the time of Nero, the Praetorian was being paid nearly three-and-a-half times as much as the legionary. Besides this there were huge bonuses, often equivalent to five years' pay, handed out by new emperors to secure the loyalty of the Guard. It was the refusal to pay this that cost Galba his life.

As might be expected, the avarice of the Guard increased with every emperor. By the end of the 2nd century AD, after the assassination of Commodus, the Guard auctioned the Empire to the highest bidder from the battlements of the Praetorian camp.

The Praetorians had their own very distinctive standards which carried images of the Emperor and his family. Their dress uniform, like the royal guards of today, was of traditional type, echoing the armour of the Republican era. The Praetorian Guard had no first centurion. Their camp lay on the outskirts of the city and later formed part of the 3rd century walls.

The Urban Cohorts

The Urban Cohorts were also within the city. They were a sort of police force under the command of the city prefect (*praefectus urbanus*). Although completely separate from the Guard, recruits sometimes joined up in order to get into the Praetorians later. The city had three of these cohorts, each 1000 strong. As they were formed at the same time as the Praetorian cohorts they were numbered 10-12.

Fire service and night police

The *vigiles* were a semi-military force founded by Augustus. They were formed into seven cohorts of 1000 men each. They were a fire service and night police for the 14 districts of Rome. A *praefectus vigilum* commanded them.

Above: A Montefortino type helmet with the inscription AVRELIVS VICTORINVS MIL COH XII VRB—*Aurelius Victorinus of the twelfth urban cohort. The survival of this type of helmet confirms that the city guards wore traditional Republican armour.*
Below: A helmet from Herculaneum, possibly of the type used by vigiles.

The Life of a Legionary

Imperial crown offered to a drunkard

Galba had been an austere man and not given to generosity. He was not popular with the army. When, in spite of their efforts, Galba became Emperor, the legions of northern Germany refused to swear allegiance to him. Again they offered the crown to their own commander and again Verginius declined. But this time he was not quite fast enough in his refusal and Galba had him recalled. The legions would still not submit to Galba. They begged the Senate to name another emperor—any other emperor.

Above: Legionary recruits training in the via quintana.

Recruitment

A legionary had to be recommended by someone connected with the army. If accepted, he received a small sum of money to cover travelling expenses to his legion. When he arrived at the camp he took the military oath. He was then posted to a century. The oath was resworn every New Year's Day.

Training

The new recruit was taught to march: during his years of service he would be expected to go on a 30-kilometre route march three times a month. He was taught how to build a camp and was drilled twice a day. (The fully-trained legionary had to drill once a day.) He was given a general training in stone slinging, swimming and riding. He learned to vault on to horseback and to mount and dismount fully armed, with shield, from either side—quite a feat before stirrups appeared. However, his main training was in the use of weapons.

Weapons training

A wooden stake about the height of a man was set up. The recruit was armed with a wicker shield and wooden sword, both of twice standard weight, and attacked the stake, learning to thrust. He also learned to throw an overweight *pilum* at the stake. Mock battles were then arranged for which both sword and *pilum* had their points covered to avoid serious accidents.

Pay and conditions

Legionaries served for 25 years. They were paid about three times as much as auxiliaries. Large monetary rewards were paid after a victory, or when a new emperor came to the throne. Soldiers were not supposed to marry, but this ruling was often ignored; at the end of the 2nd century AD it was dropped. On retirement, the legionary was given a choice of a land grant or a sum of money. A retired legionary would usually settle in the land where he had served.

The Standards

There were three main types of standard. The *aquila* (eagle) was the standard of the whole legion. It was introduced when the legions became permanent units. By Caesar's time it was made of silver and gold. During the Empire it was made entirely of gold. The eagle never left camp unless the whole legion set out. It was guarded by the first cohort.

There were still standards for each individual century (*signa*) as there had been during the Republic. The legion also carried a portrait of the Emperor (*imago*) and sometimes a legion symbol, usually a sign of the zodiac.

There were also special flags (*vexilla*) for detachments serving away from the legion.

The standards were carried on poles pointed at the bottom so they could be stuck in the ground. The pole also had handles with which to pull it up. In camp, the standards were kept in a special chapel in the *principia*.

Soon after his accession, Galba had appointed Aulus Vitellius governor of southern Germany. It was a terrible choice. Although of the noblest blood, Vitellius was a glutton and a drunkard. It was to this man that the German legions now offered the crown. Verginius had refused because of his humble background. Vitellius felt no such humility.

News of Galba's death reached Germany too late. Three armies were already on the march. The one from northern Germany was made up mainly of Legion *V Alaudae* plus detachments from the other legions, reinforced by cavalry units. They plundered and looted their way through France. A second army from southern Germany, composed of Legion *XXI Rapax* plus other legionary detachments, advanced directly on Italy. These armies were strongly supported by savage German auxiliaries. They totalled about 70,000 men. A third army commanded by Vitellius himself brought up the rear.

Otho reaped the harvest of his treachery; he inherited Galba's war. He sent desperate messages to the Danube legions. Then, gathering all available forces, including the Praetorian and Urban Cohorts, he marched north to meet Vitellius.

Signum
Aquila
Vexillum

1
2
4
3
5

1. Reconstructions of legion standards.
2. An eagle from the time of Caesar.
3. Standards from Trajan's Column.
4. Remains of a vexillum *from Egypt.*
5. A legion symbol.

Religion

The Roman soldier was very superstitious. He was careful not to offend any of the supernatural powers which influenced his life. It therefore comes as no surprise to find the soldiers worshipping a multitude of gods including the local god of the area where his legion was camped.

Certain religions were more popular with the soldiers than others. There is no evidence of Christianity in the army during the 1st century AD, probably because the early Christians were strict pacifists.

However, there are many examples of Mithraism. This was an essentially masculine religion which gloried in feats of strength and endurance and therefore appealed to the soldiers.

Unifying spirits

The Romans believed in *genii*, unifying spirits which bonded groups of people together; the group might be a mere family, a legion or a nation. In the legions these spirits were personified quite naturally in the standards. It is for this reason that the standards were so revered and that it was such a disgrace to lose a standard in battle.

Leisure

The legionary of the early Empire was often recruited from the urban populations and tried to bring the pleasures of town life to the camp.

The traditional Roman bath buildings are found on or near most camps. These bath buildings had various rooms for hot, cold and tepid baths. There were also exercise and massage rooms. The baths were used as clubs by both soldier and civilian alike.

All camps also seem to have had an amphitheatre, either within or just outside the walls.

The Officers

Vespasian enters the contest

The eastern provinces watched this series of events with astonishment, as one rival claimant after another vied for supreme power.

In the last years of Nero's reign the Jews had revolted and the Emperor had dispatched Vespasian, an able general, to suppress the insurrection. Vespasian had quickly conquered Galilee and was preparing to besiege the last insurgents who had taken refuge in Jerusalem, when he heard of Nero's death. He sent his son Titus to congratulate Galba on his accession to the throne. On his way Titus

The Centurions

A legionary signed on for 25 years. He might hope to rise to the rank of centurion in this time. The centurionate covered all the lower and middle ranking commissioned officers in the legion.

During the Republic these officers had been elected each year by the soldiers. Now they were nominated on a permanent basis by the *legatus*. Although they usually rose from the ranks, centurions were sometimes appointed directly from civilian life. Each legion had 59 centurions.

On the ranking of centurions, the old names of *hastatus*, *princeps* and *triarius* (under its alternative title of *pilus*) still survived. There were six centurions to each of the second to tenth cohorts; they were *hastatus posterior*, *hastatus prior*, *princeps posterior*, *princeps prior*, *pilus posterior*, *pilus prior*. The number of the cohort would be placed before each of these names; for example, *Decimus Hastatus Posterior* came from the tenth cohort. The centurion with the greatest seniority commanded his cohort.

Armour

A centurion's armour was silvered. He wore greaves, and the crest on his helmet was turned so that it ran across the helmet from side to side. His sword and dagger were worn on the opposite sides to those of the legionary.

Brutality and corruption

Centurions were often brutal; many a legionary could show scars on his back from the centurion's vine cane. They were not above taking bribes from legionaries who wished to avoid some duty. Bribery became so common that even the Emperor dared not stop it; thus we find the Emperor paying up the soldiers' debts in order to obtain their allegiance.

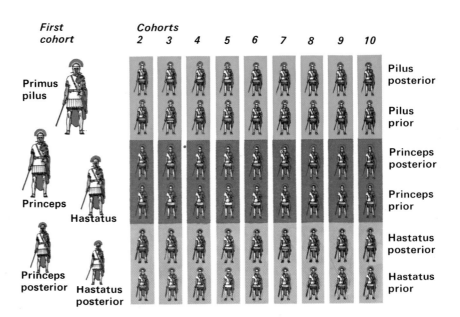

Primi ordines

The first cohort was divided into five double centuries. The five centurions of this cohort were known as *primi ordines*. They outranked all other centurions in the legions.

Within the *primi ordines*, the ascending order of superiority was as follows: *hastatus posterior*, *princeps posterior*, *hastatus*, *princeps* and *primus pilus* who was the highest ranking centurion in the legion.

Primus pilus

The rank of *primus pilus* was the dream of every legionary but to most it was impossible, for this rank demanded considerable educational and administrative ability.

The rank could only be held for one year, after which the centurion either retired or moved on to better things. M Pompeius Asper, for example, after being *primus pilus* in Legion III Cyrenaica moved on to be *praefectus castrorum* in Legion XX Valeria Victrix.

Above: The centurionate. The centurions of Cohorts 2–10 rose in seniority but did not normally change position. Promotion was to hastatus posterior of the first cohort and from there in four steps to primus pilus.

Above: The tombstone of the centurion T Calidius Severus showing his scale cuirass, greaves, transverse crested helmet and vine cane.

heard of the death of Galba and returned to Palestine. Vespasian viewed the events engulfing the Empire with distaste. When his troops hailed him as Emperor he paused only long enough to ensure the support of the Syrian and Egyptian legions before he accepted the crown, adding yet another name to the list of contestants.

In the west, however, province after province declared for Vitellius; all the western legions from Britain to Spain supported him. About 100,000 men invaded Italy. Otho was unable to collect anywhere near this number. Although detachments from the Danube legions arrived in time, most of this army missed the battle. The Othonian army was cut to pieces near Cremona, in the Po valley. The survivors escaped to the fortress at Bedriacum nearby, but surrendered the next day. Otho committed suicide, dying with more dignity than he had lived.

It was several weeks after the battle that Vitellius arrived to receive his crown. He showed clemency to the senior officers of the defeated army. However, he treated several of the centurions from the Danube legions with particular brutality, an action he would soon regret.

Tribunes

Above the centurionate was a group of semi-professional officers. The tribunes came first. There were still six of these to each legion. They generally held their post only as a step in their political career.

The chief tribune (*tribunus laticlavius*) was an aristocrat who served a short term with the army before entering the Senate at the age of 25. He was identified by a broad purple band on his tunic. The other tribunes (*tribuni angusticlavii*) were from the upper-middle class (*equites*) and usually held only administrative positions within the legion. Their tunics bore a narrow purple band.

Legion Commander and camp prefect

Above the tribunes was the *legatus* who was usually a senator appointed to his position by the Emperor. There was one other high ranking officer, the camp prefect (*praefectus castrorum*). He was normally an older man who had been *primus pilus* and whose whole life had been spent in the army. The *praefectus castrorum* commanded the legion in the absence of the *legatus* and senior tribune.

Other officers

Below the centurionate, the main officers were the *principales*. These included the *optio*, who was the centurion's second-in-command; the standard bearers, among whom each legion had one *aquilifer* who bore the eagle; and one *signifer* for each century who also acted as his unit's banker.

There were also trumpeters (*cornicines*), guard commanders (*tesserarii*), intelligence officers (*frumentarii*), torturers (*quaestionarii*) and executioners (*speculatores*). Besides these there were veterinary surgeons, doctors, clerks and other specialists.

Above: Vespasian reviews his officers.
1. A centurion.
2. A signifer *with an aquilifer behind.*
3. A horn blower (cornicen) *with a trumpeter* (tubicen) *behind him.*
4. A tribune.
5. Vespasian as commander-in-chief. In the background can be seen the rods and axes of the lictors.

47

Legionary Armour

Above: Legionaries wearing plate armour (from Trajan's Column).

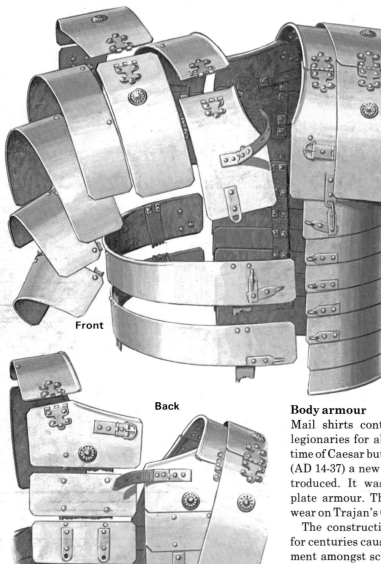

Front

Back

Above right: Pieces of Roman plate armour found at Corbridge.

Above: A reconstruction of the Corbridge hook-type plate armour.

Main shoulder unit

Chest and upper back unit

Bunch of waist girdle plates

Body armour

Mail shirts continued to be worn by legionaries for about 80 years after the time of Caesar but late in Tiberius's reign (AD 14-37) a new type of armour was introduced. It was the first articulated plate armour. This is what legionaries wear on Trajan's Column.

The construction of this armour has for centuries caused a great deal of argument amongst scholars. In 1964, at Corbridge on Hadrian's Wall, two complete sets of this armour were excavated. They showed two similar types. Reconstructions of these have been made by Mr H. Russell Robinson of the Tower of London and it is thanks to his work that we now know in every detail how this type of armour was made.

Two types

The chest and upper back plates were attached to the lower part of the armour in two ways. One type was hooked; the other type (not illustrated) was joined with straps and buckles only; these were on the outside at the front and on the inside at the back.

On both types, the chest and upper back plates were joined by straps and buckles. The segments of the chest and shoulder units were joined with decorative hinges. On one example, where the hinge had broken, the two pieces had been riveted together. The narrow bands on shoulders, waist and upper back were riveted to leather strapping. The waist bands were laced together at front and back.

Evolution of the legionary helmet in the 1st century AD

1. Gallic; bronze; 3rd/1st centuries BC

2. Germany; bronze; early 1st century AD

3. Alsace; bronze; mid-1st century AD

4. Gallic; iron; mid-1st century BC

5. Holland; iron; late 1st century BC

6. Germany; iron and bronze; mid-1st century AD

7. Holland; silvered bronze; early 1st century AD

8. Italy; bronze; mid-1st century AD

9. Italy; bronze; mid-1st century AD

10. Germany; iron and bronze; 2nd half 1st century AD

11. Israel; iron and bronze; early 2nd century AD

1-3. Jockey Cap type; disappears mid-1st century AD.
4-6. Imperial Gallic type.
7-11. Italian types.

Helmets

Shortly after the conquest of Gaul, the northern legions phased out their old-style helmets, the Montefortino (**7** above) and Etrusco-Corinthian types, and adopted Gallic types (**1** and **4**).

From these they derived the type known as the Jockey Cap (**2** and **3**) and later the Imperial Gallic helmet (**6**) which had the neck guard lowered to protect the neck and shoulders. Finally, at the end of the first century AD, the famous "Hot Cross Bun" helmet (**11**) was introduced. These can be seen on Trajan's Column.

The development of the helmet in Italy was far more conservative. The Montefortino type continued in use among the imperial guards and even when the "Jockey Cap" was introduced it retained many of the characteristics of the Montefortino (see **8**).

Craftsmanship

The Gallic helmets are of a far higher standard of workmanship than the Italian ones. With the exception of the Jockey Cap type they are usually iron whereas the Italians continue to use mainly bronze. **9** above is a crude Italian version of the Imperial Gallic type (**6**). **10** is also of Italian origin and is a proto-type for the Trajanic helmets (**11**).

Helmets **8** and **9** were found in the river Po and were probably lost by soldiers of Otho's army after their defeat at Cremona.

Legionary Equipment

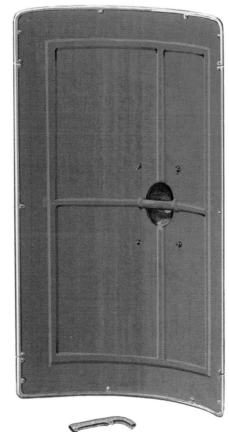

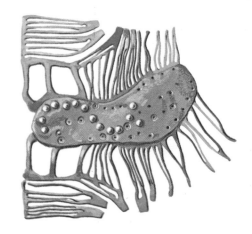

Above: A bronze shield boss belonging to Junius Dubitatus who served in Britain with a detachment from Legion VIII Augusta, in the 2nd century AD. Scale 1:5.

Below: The remains of a military sandal. The loops of leather were laced up the foot and ankle.

Left: Front view of the shield from Dura Europos. Scale 1:10.

Above: The inside of a 1st century AD legionary shield reconstructed from the Dura Europos shield. Below it is a piece of bronze shield-binding.

Shields

The rectangular shield was introduced early in the 1st century AD. At first this was just the old oval *scutum* shorn off at the top and bottom, but later the sides were also squared off. The only surviving example comes from Dura Europos in Syria, dating from the 3rd century AD.

This shield is constructed of three layers of thin strips of plane wood about 2 millimetres thick, glued across each other to form a curved piece of plywood. The back is strengthened with strips of wood which are also glued on. The handle is formed by thickening the central one of these strips. The hand grip was fronted with an iron or bronze boss similar to the type shown above.

The whole is encased in leather and the front is covered with a layer of linen. The edges are bound with rawhide stitched through the wood (in the 1st and 2nd centuries bronze binding was used). It is worth comparing the construction of this shield with the one shown on page 18.

The shields shown on sculptures usually have decorations on them. A passage from Tacitus describing the second battle of Cremona tells us how two legionaries picked up shields from their fallen enemies and, hiding behind these, managed to infiltrate the enemy lines and put a catapult out of action. As this was at night with only the moon shining, it suggests that the motifs painted on the shields were a way of identifying a unit.

Belts

Early in the 1st century AD, the sword and dagger were suspended from two individual belts which crossed over at the back and front cowboy fashion. An apron of metal discs, riveted to leather straps, hung from these belts.

Later a single belt, to which the dagger and apron were attached, was substituted. The sword was suspended from a baldric. These belts were covered with rectangular metal plates, usually of silvered bronze. Examples of belt plates have been found on most legionary sites, including Numantia, dating them back to the 2nd century BC.

Sandals

Many examples of military sandals (*caligae*) have been discovered. The upper was cut from a single piece of leather which wrapped around the foot and was sewn up at the heel. This was attached to a heavy sole made of several layers of leather. The sole was shod with iron studs.

Josephus describes a centurion dashing across the paved temple courtyard at Jerusalem, skidding on these iron studs and falling flat on his back.

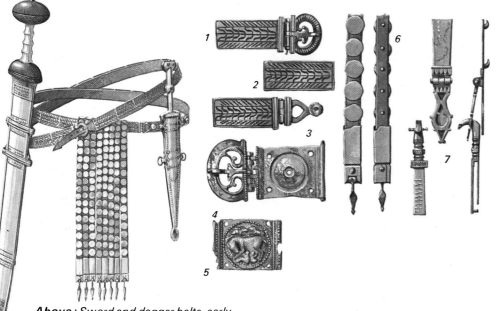

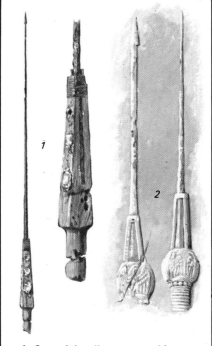

1. *One of the* pila *recovered from Oberraden. Scale 1:10.*
2. *The weighted* pila *shown on the Cancelleria relief.*

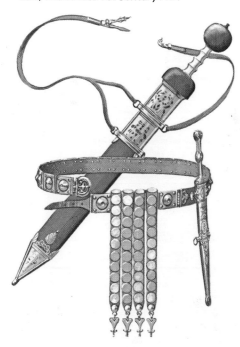

Above: *Sword and dagger belts, early 1st century AD.*

Above right: *Archaeological examples of belt and baldric pieces of the 1st century AD.*

1-3. *Buckle, belt plate and dagger frog from double belts.*
4. *Belt buckle from single belt.*
5. *Decorated belt plate with Romulus motif.*
6. *Apron strap, back and front.*
7. *Pair of baldric fasteners. All pieces come from Germany. All are bronze and most show traces of tinning.*

Below: *Sword with baldric and dagger belt, mid to late 1st century AD.*

The pilum

Several *pila* survive from this period. The best examples are from Oberraden in northern Germany. In these, not only the iron but also part of the wooden shaft survives (see **1** right). It is similar to the heavy *pilum* of previous periods with a flat iron tang held to the wooden shaft by two rivets. However, it is of much lighter construction than those from Numantia.

Possibly because of the lightening of the *pilum*, a heavier javelin was introduced in the middle of the 1st century AD. It had a round lead weight inserted at the junction of wood and iron. This type is shown on a relief (see **2** right) from the time of Domitian (AD 81-96); unfortunately we have no certain archaeological specimens of this type.

The sword

We have a dozen or so well preserved swords from this period. In the first part of the century, swords still echoed the dagger shape of the early Spanish swords and had a long tapering point (see **3** right). Later in the century the sides became parallel and the point shorter. Three examples of the latter type have been recovered from Pompeii (see **5** right). The scabbards were usually made of wood and leather held together with bronze.

The dagger

Several daggers survive from this period. They vary little in shape, though some have longer points than others. The scabbards are made of bronze (**6** right) or iron. They are often highly decorated with silver inlay (**8** right). The dagger seems to have disappeared from legionary equipment at the end of the 1st century AD. Not a single example is shown on Trajan's Column.

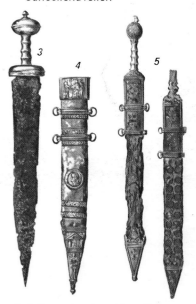

3-4. *Sword and scabbard from Germany.*
5. *Two swords from Pompeii.*
6. *Dagger from Holland.*
7. *Dagger from Germany.*
8. *Dagger scabbard from Germany.*

On the March

Vespasian's army advances

In the east, Vespasian prepared for war. He put his son Titus in charge of the Jewish war and retired to Egypt to cut off Rome's food supply. Messages were sent to the Praetorians who had been disbanded by Vitellius, promising them reinstatement. Mucianus, Vespasian's chief lieutenant, set out on the long march to Italy with Legion *VI Ferrata* plus about 13,000 re-enlisted veterans.

The Danube legions were still enraged by the treatment of their centurions after the battle of Cremona. As Vespasian's army advanced through

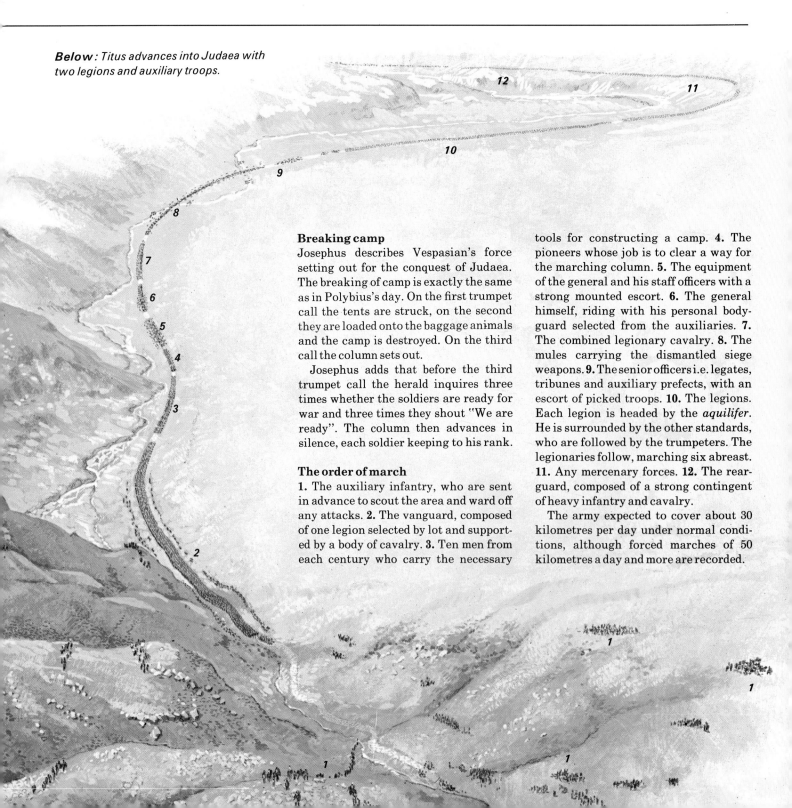

Below: Titus advances into Judaea with two legions and auxiliary troops.

Breaking camp

Josephus describes Vespasian's force setting out for the conquest of Judaea. The breaking of camp is exactly the same as in Polybius's day. On the first trumpet call the tents are struck, on the second they are loaded onto the baggage animals and the camp is destroyed. On the third call the column sets out.

Josephus adds that before the third trumpet call the herald inquires three times whether the soldiers are ready for war and three times they shout "We are ready". The column then advances in silence, each soldier keeping to his rank.

The order of march

1. The auxiliary infantry, who are sent in advance to scout the area and ward off any attacks. **2.** The vanguard, composed of one legion selected by lot and supported by a body of cavalry. **3.** Ten men from each century who carry the necessary tools for constructing a camp. **4.** The pioneers whose job is to clear a way for the marching column. **5.** The equipment of the general and his staff officers with a strong mounted escort. **6.** The general himself, riding with his personal bodyguard selected from the auxiliaries. **7.** The combined legionary cavalry. **8.** The mules carrying the dismantled siege weapons. **9.** The senior officers i.e. legates, tribunes and auxiliary prefects, with an escort of picked troops. **10.** The legions. Each legion is headed by the *aquilifer*. He is surrounded by the other standards, who are followed by the trumpeters. The legionaries follow, marching six abreast. **11.** Any mercenary forces. **12.** The rearguard, composed of a strong contingent of heavy infantry and cavalry.

The army expected to cover about 30 kilometres per day under normal conditions, although forced marches of 50 kilometres a day and more are recorded.

Syria and Turkey, they rose in his support. Antoninus Primus, the legate of Legion *VII Claudia*, advanced into Italy ahead of Mucianus at the head of a small army of light-armed auxiliaries. His aim was to secure the eastern passes of the Alps.

Meanwhile, Italy was subjected to the lusts of Vitellius and the German army for five months. This vast horde of soldiers and camp followers pillaged the towns and villages in their search for delicacies for the Emperor's table. Barbaric German horsemen trampled the fields of Tuscany and the countryside was devastated. Farmers hid their wives and children, fearing the lusts of the soldiers. Bloody quarrels broke out between legionaries and auxiliaries. The armies had camped outside Rome but, even so, the city became packed with soldiers searching for pleasure. Disease broke out and many of the auxiliaries, unused to urban life, died.

News of trouble in the east arrived but was suppressed; nothing was allowed to interfere with the Emperor's pleasure. Vitellius feasted and fêted his soldiers with games, circuses and gladiatorial contests, completely oblivious to the storm clouds rising in the east.

Baggage

Besides armour and weapons, each legionary carried a saw, pickaxe, sickle, basket, bucket, chain, strap and at least three days' rations. Sometimes the rations might be as much as 15 days' supply. This was all carried on a pole over his shoulder. A mule was allocated to each eight men to carry their tent and any surplus equipment. Baggage was normally carried by mules or in carts. However, on Trajan's Column soldiers are shown loading their equipment into boats to be carried along the Danube.

When the army approached a fordable river, half the cavalry entered the water upstream and the other half downstream. The infantry and baggage train crossed between them. The group upstream broke the force of the current and that downstream caught any equipment that got carried away by the river.

Diet

The soldier's basic diet on campaign was wheat baked in the form of hard wholemeal biscuits. This was supplemented by bacon, cheese and sour wine, all preserved types of food. However, excavations at military sites show that, in camp at least, the Roman soldier had a very varied diet including beef, mutton, pork and other meats. Poultry, eggs, fish and shellfish were also eaten as were a great variety of fruit and vegetables. Salt was considered a necessity.

Above: **1.** Legionaries carrying their baggage. **2.** Legionary with his equipment in his shield (from Trajan's Column).

Above: **1.** Leather shield cover. **2.** Pieces of tent leather. **3.** Palisade stake (all from northern Britain). **4-5.** Bucket and mess tin from Cremona. **6.** Figure-eight chain from Numantia.

Right: Eight legionaries lowering their tent and preparing to march.

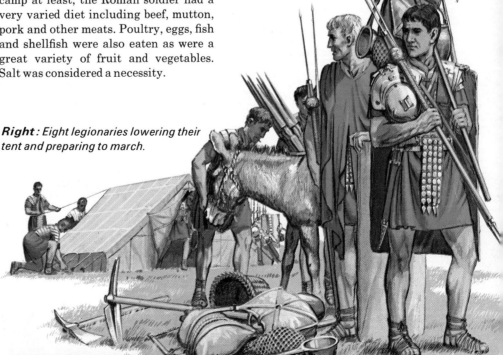

Auxiliary Infantry

The pleasures of Vitellius and his followers were rudely interrupted when Primus arrived in northeast Italy in command of a small force of auxiliaries. He had been sent by Vespasian to secure the alpine passes in advance of the Danube legions. In panic, Vitellius sent for reinforcements from Germany and Britain but none came. Only Legion *III Augusta* in North Africa expressed open support for him. His troops had become an undisciplined rabble.

Nevertheless the German legions marched northward and occupied Hostilia and Cremona, the two

Above: *Various types of auxiliary are shown on Trajan's Column. However, the majority are of the type shown on the right.*

Auxiliaries

The term *auxilia* was applied to all units other than the legions. These included cavalry and all types of light infantry. Ever since the time of Hannibal, auxiliary soldiers with special skills, such as Cretan archers and Balearic slingers, had served with the army. In the early Empire they had been formed into regular regiments of 500 strong. Late in the 1st century AD some units of 1,000 men appeared.

As with the legionaries, these auxiliary units were referred to as cohorts and, again as in the legions, they were split up into centuries commanded by centurions. The cohort itself was commanded by a Roman prefect.

Organization

Auxiliaries were originally formed from the frontier populations to fight in their own area, using their local knowledge. However, as in all Roman organizations, there was a tendency to formalize. Units adopted a standard equipment and were posted abroad, thus defeating their original purpose. New local units were constantly needed.

These forces were mainly used for frontier skirmishes, taking the weight of this work from the legionaries. Judging from the number of auxiliary forts, there must have been almost as many auxiliaries as legionaries. On Trajan's Column we find auxiliary infantry, cavalry, bowmen and slingers.

crossing points of the river Po. The main army, two legions and detachments from four German and three British legions plus auxiliaries, was stationed at Hostilia. A much smaller force garrisoned the colony at Cremona. Valens was the commander of the Vitellian forces. Having secured the line of the Po against invasion, he crossed the Alps to southern France to arrange for reinforcements. The army was left without a commander.

Meanwhile Primus was at Patavium, about 50 kilometres from the Po, with his force of auxiliaries. His original orders had been to secure the passes of the eastern Alps and await the arrival of Mucianus. But while Valens was securing the line of the Po, Primus had been joined by two of the Danube legions. Now, in defiance of his orders, he moved his expanded force to Verona, about 45 kilometres from Hostilia. In this way, Primus covered the Brenner Pass, cutting off the route of any Vitellian reinforcements from Germany.

Primus was joined at Verona by a further three Danubian legions, leaving that frontier, like the Rhine, defended only by a skeleton legionary force and a string of under-manned auxiliary forts.

Scale 1:1

Above: Bronze scale armour. The scales were wired together then sewn to a fabric lining through the centre holes. Scales vary in size from 1-5 cms. long.

Above: During the Empire mail was made of alternate lines of punched rings (1) joined by riveted rings (2).

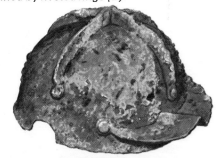

Above: Early 2nd century auxiliary helmet. The neckguard has been cut off.

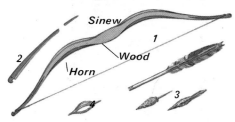

1. Composite bow. 2. Horn nock. 3. Parts of arrows. 4. Fire-brand arrow head.

Pay and conditions

The auxiliary infantryman served in the army for 25 years. On his discharge he received a grant of Roman citizenship. This grant was inscribed on a pair of bronze sheets known as a *diploma*. Many of these have been found on excavations. An example of one of them is given on the right.

Auxiliary infantry pay was probably only about one-third of the amount that the legionary received.

Soldiers' children

Like the legionary, the auxiliary was not allowed to marry. However, the grant of citizenship given at the end of service extended to his children. These then became eligible for service in the legions. The illegitimate children of a legionary did not have this right.

Armour

Although some auxiliaries wore no armour, those who did wore either mail or scale armour. Scale armour was made by sewing overlapping rows of metal scales onto a linen undergarment. The cut of these cuirasses was much the same as the mail ones. The helmets of the auxiliaries were usually cheap versions of the current legionary types.

Weapons

The weapons of the mailed infantry were usually a sword, similar to the legionary *gladius*, and a short spear.

Archers were usually of eastern origin, and they used the composite bow. This bow was much smaller than the famed English long bow and was made of wood strengthened on the inside of the curve with horn and on the outside with sinew. A pair of horn nocks reinforced each end and to these the string was attached. Many horn nocks have been found on Roman military sites.

Above: A diploma from Trajan granting citizenship to M Spedius Corbulo on his completion of 25 years' service as an auxiliary.

Below: A painted auxiliary shield from Dura Europos. Scale 1:14.

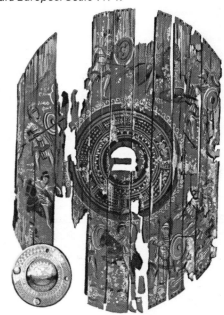

Frontier Defences

Primus arrives at Cremona

Primus had already exceeded his orders by advancing into the valley of the Po. Now the soldiers refused to fortify their position and demanded to be led against the enemy. Pushed on by his soldiers, Primus advanced on Cremona hoping to force a battle with the smaller part of the Vitellian forces while their commander was absent.

Meanwhile, unaware of Primus's plans, the dispirited Vitellian forces in Hostilia decided to join their fellows at Cremona, leaving open the route to Rome. But Primus had already gone. In two days he

Military colonies

Colonization meant the settling of groups of soldiers at strategic points in newly-conquered territory. The purpose was two-fold: to act as strongholds in the event of revolt and to "Romanize" the local population. Colonies served Rome well in her war with Hannibal, giving her a long chain of fortified posts inside Carthaginian-held territory.

In the Republic, every eligible citizen was also a soldier, and colonies were formed from those on the military roll. Later they were formed from retired veterans.

The colony was divided up into lots one *centuria* (about 700 metres) square. This was farmed by four families. "Centuriation" was practised over the whole Roman world. Even today the system of square plots shows up on aerial photographs and may sometimes be seen clearly in the road systems on maps.

The site at ancient Capua (below) is interesting because it was colonized at about the same time as Cremona which was set up to control the Gauls of the Po valley in the year that Hannibal crossed the Alps, 218 BC.

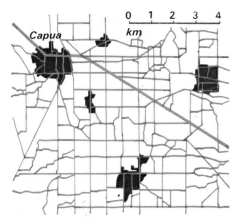

Above: *Map of ancient Capua showing the roads and paths that still follow the Roman centuriation grid.*

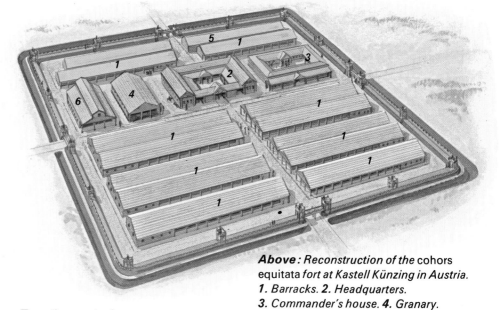

Above: *Reconstruction of the* cohors equitata *fort at Kastell Künzing in Austria.*
1. Barracks. 2. Headquarters.
3. Commander's house. 4. Granary.
5. Stables. 6. Hospital.

Below: *A reconstruction of a watch/signal tower from Trajan's Column.*

Frontier control

When Augustus became Emperor he inherited an unwieldy mixture of races. Most had been under Roman control for less than 50 years. He made some conquests but spent most of his long reign trying to organize his inheritance. When he lay dying he begged Tiberius not to try to extend the Empire but to continue his work of consolidation.

Apart from the invasion of Britain in AD 43, this was the policy of all the emperors of the 1st century. When Trajan came to the throne in AD 98, the Empire was hardly different in extent from that which Augustus had taken over 130 years before.

The Romans believed that one day the Empire would be extended both in the north and east. For this reason, no formal borders were drawn. The frontier zones were controlled by a series of auxiliary forts backed up by the legionary fortresses which were usually some distance back from the frontier.

had reached the site of Otho's defeat. The next morning he sent forward his cavalry to try and force a battle. He himself arrived at Cremona in the afternoon with the five legions. His troops clamoured to be led against the town.

By this time, the other half of the Vitellian army had heard of Primus's march and was racing towards Cremona. They arrived at nightfall, having covered 30 miles during the day. Primus was far from his base and unable to fortify a camp. He had no alternative but to offer battle. He drew up his forces on either side of the road; he was massively outnumbered.

Above: A reconstruction of Hadrian's Wall showing turret 41a. Mile castle 41 is in the distance.

Below: A reconstruction of a wall turret from the Rhine-Danube defences in Bavaria.

The barbarian threat
For some years Rome had been troubled by barbarians invading across the Danube. There was also a periodic threat from Parthia in the east. Trajan invaded both these areas and extended the Empire to include Romania in the north and the Persian Gulf in the east.

When Trajan died in AD 117 he left the Empire at its greatest extent. His successor, Hadrian, decided that this disjointed mass was impossible to govern effectively. He abandoned most of Trajan's conquests and erected a rigid frontier defence system, aiming not to control the frontier people but to exclude them.

The Rhine defences
Hadrian made the Rhine the frontier from Bonn to the sea. A series of auxiliary forts and the legionary fortresses fortified the west bank. These were supported by signal and watch towers, as may be seen on Trajan's Column.

The link with the Danube
The river Danube was similarly fortified from Regensburg to the Black Sea. A ditch and palisade were constructed from a point just south of Bonn to one near Regensburg to join the two rivers.

These fortifications stretched for about 450 kilometres. They were reinforced by a fort every 8-10 kilometres. In places towards the Danube the palisade was replaced by a wall with turrets.

The defence of the east and south remained much the same as before.

Hadrian's Wall
In northern Britain Hadrian erected his most lasting monument: the wall that bears his name. It was 2.5 metres thick and 5 metres high. It stretched for nearly 120 kilometres, defended by 80 small mile-castles 1.6 kilometres apart and about 160 turrets. Like the Rhine-Danube defences, Hadrian's Wall also had a fort every 8-10 kilometres.

The Cavalry

Mucianus was far behind Primus. Both he and Vespasian had sent letters to the headstrong commander of the Danube legions. They begged him to show caution and to be content to hold the passes of the Alps until the rest of the army could be brought up. Their pleas were to no avail.

The barbarian tribes saw that the frontiers had no defenders and rose in revolt on both the Rhine and the Danube. Hordes of savage tribesmen, accompanied by heavy armed Sarmatian cavalry, poured across the Danube into the Empire. These Sarmatian

Above: A horseman from the Aemilius Paullus monument at Delphi, first half of the 2nd century BC.
Right: A cavalryman from the Altar of Domitius Ahenobarbus, mid-1st century BC. He definitely wears a mail shirt.

Cavalry

The weakest link in the Roman army had always been the cavalry. When Hannibal invaded Italy, his Spanish and African cavalry were the key to his success. At the great Battle of Cannae (216 BC) the Carthaginian horsemen drove the Roman cavalry right off the field of battle. Hannibal could then attack the legions from the flanks, with devastating results.

At the Battle of Pydna the Romans had only 600 cavalry; their allies supplied three times that number. 25 years later the Romans dropped citizen cavalry altogether. Instead they employed contingents of horsemen supplied and led by the local chiefs in the areas of operation. We find Caesar employing Gallic and German cavalry units against Pompey in the civil war.

Organization

Early in the Empire these cavalry units had been organized into regiments (*alae*) of 500 strong. As with the infantry, units of 1,000 appear towards the end of the 1st century AD. These *alae* were divided into units (*turmae*) of about 30 or 40 strong. Each *turma* was commanded by a decurion.

Although the squadrons themselves had originally been commanded by their own chieftains they were now commanded by Roman prefects. Each *alae* had its own flag (*vexillum*) and each *turma* had a standard (*signum*).

It has been suggested that the Romans did not employ armoured cavalry until the beginning of the 2nd century AD. This opinion is based upon a misinterpretation of the monuments.

Painted sculpture

As we have seen, the Romans painted their sculpture and so the lack of mail shown on horsemen on Trajan's Column and other monuments and tombstones is not surprising. Legionary tombstones of the first hundred years of the Empire do not show mail either and yet there is no question that the legionaries of this period wore a coat of mail.

Evidence

The cavalrymen on the Aemilius Paullus monument are wearing cuirasses cut in exactly the same way as the legionaries, who are certainly wearing mail. There is a horseman on the Ahenobarbus Relief from the time of Caesar who is wearing clearly-depicted mail.

There is a very detailed sculpture from Mantua, dating from late in the reign of Augustus, which shows two cavalrymen, one in mail and one in scale armour and there are many 1st century cavalry tombstones from Germany showing body armour cut to the same pattern.

There are cavalrymen on the Trajanic Frieze from the Arch of Constantine, (AD 115). They are also wearing mail, and, incidentally, the cut of their cuirasses is exactly the same as those of the cavalrymen on Trajan's Column.

The Lacus Curtius Relief from Rome showing a Republican horseman with round shield (parma equestris).

horsemen had migrated to the Danube from the steppes of southern Russia, and they wrought havoc amongst the lighter armed Roman cavalry. Mucianus was forced to halt and send part of his army northwards to drive these barbarians back across the river.

Fortune now smiled on Primus again. The Vitellian army should have rested for the night at Cremona. This would have left Primus and his troops the task of trying to fortify a camp in the plain, far from their base and constantly harassed by enemy cavalry. But Vitellius's undisciplined soldiers, although worn out by their long march and without a commander, attacked nevertheless.

All night long the battle raged. The moon rose behind Primus's troops giving them the advantage of fighting from the shadows. The fortunes of the battle passed from side to side.

At dawn one of the eastern legions sent up a shout of praise for the sun, as was their custom. The Vitellians, believing that Mucianus had arrived, broke ranks, fled for Cremona and crowded into the camp. This had been built beneath the walls of the town by the two legions who had been sent to garrison the colony.

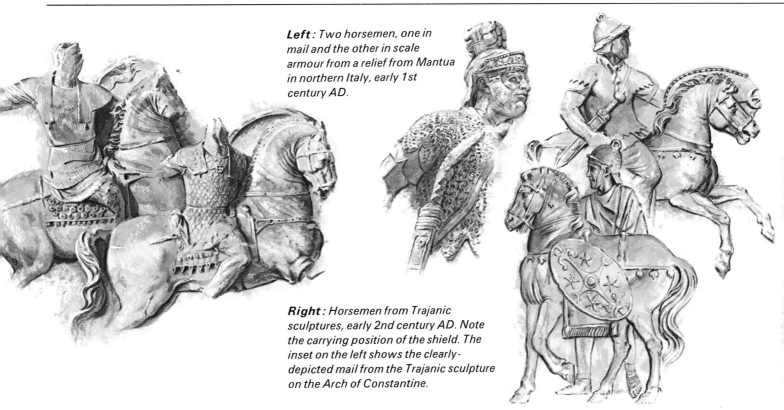

Left: Two horsemen, one in mail and the other in scale armour from a relief from Mantua in northern Italy, early 1st century AD.

Right: Horsemen from Trajanic sculptures, early 2nd century AD. Note the carrying position of the shield. The inset on the left shows the clearly-depicted mail from the Trajanic sculpture on the Arch of Constantine.

Development of armoured cavalry
Armoured cavalry had developed in the Middle East about 900-800 BC. Horse armour, found in both Italy and Greece, dating from the 5th-4th century BC, shows that armoured cavalry was in use throughout the classical period.

Light cavalry
The Romans also used North African light cavalry. These horsemen, who had wreaked such havoc in the Roman armies during the war with Hannibal, were completely unarmoured and rode without a bridle. They were armed with javelins and light spears. Their speed and agility allowed them to charge and withdraw before their opponents could react. They must have been used well into the Empire for they appear on Trajan's Column. The Romans also used mounted archers.

Cohortes Equitatae
Caesar was very impressed by German mixed cavalry in which light armed infantrymen ran along with the horsemen holding on to the horse's mane in order to keep up. The Romans themselves had sometimes mixed their *velites* with the cavalry. This may have been the origin of the bodies of mixed troops known as *cohortes equitatae* which we find in the Empire. These were made up of roughly three-quarters infantry and one-quarter cavalry and were also organized into cohorts of 500 or 1000.

Pay
Very little is known of cavalry pay. It probably varied from light to heavy cavalry, for the armour used by the heavy cavalry both for battle and sports was very expensive.

Below: A North African light horseman. These cavalrymen rode without bridles.

Cavalry Equipment

Armour

Greek cavalrymen had worn helmets without cheek or neckguards to allow all-round vision and hearing. The Roman cavalryman however, wore a helmet that covered the whole head leaving only the eyes, nose and mouth visible. The ears were completely enclosed.

Body armour was similar to that of the auxiliaries, being of mail or scale.

In the early Empire horses wore no armour but were decorated with pendants made of bronze. Many of these have been found in excavations all over the Empire and are to be seen on many Roman sculptures and cavalry tombstones. It was not until the time of Hadrian that the *cataphractus* was introduced. For this both man and horse were heavily armoured.

Weapons of the Republic

In the later Republic the cavalrymen used a Greek spear with a pointed iron butt; if the spear broke he could use the other end. He also had a sword and a round convex shield (*parma equestris*).

Weapons of the Empire

During the early Empire a longer sword (*spatha*) was adopted, probably developed from the Celtic long sword. The shield was now either oval or hexagonal and in both cases flat. When not in action, the shield was carried alongside the horse, sometimes under the saddle blanket. Josephus tells us that Vespasian's cavalry also had a quiver of three or more darts with points as large as spears. This quiver was probably attached to the horse.

Saddles

The saddle suddenly appears for the first time in history on Roman sculptures of the early Empire. However, it can be shown that the saddle, like much Roman military equipment, was almost certainly of Celtic origin.

In his commentary on the Gallic war, Caesar casually remarks that the Germans scorned the use of the saddle. As Caesar was then employing Celtic cavalry almost exclusively, it implies that the Celts used the saddle.

Above: Vespasian's cavalry pursues the fleeing Vitellians after the Battle of Cremona.

Below: Reconstruction of late 1st century cavalry helmet and long cutting sword (spatha).

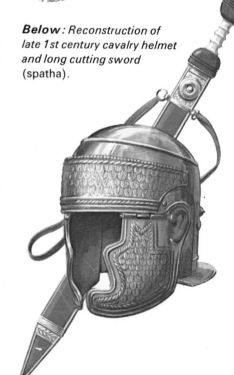

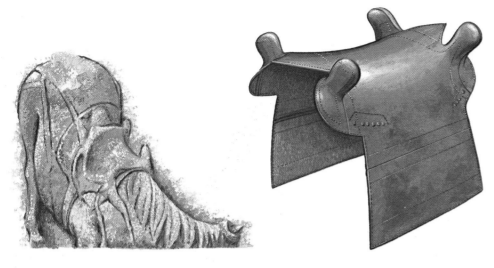

Far left: Fallen horse from the Julii monument at St Remy in southern France. Although this must be a Celtic horse and the sculpture dates from shortly after the death of Caesar, the saddle is of the type used by the Romans.

Left: A Roman saddle reconstructed from pieces found in Holland. The pommels are reinforced on the inside with bronze plates.

The St Remy Monument

At St Remy in southern France there is a monument erected shortly after the death of Caesar. This commemorates a battle involving Romans and Celts. It shows a cavalry battle in which one of the horses has fallen and thrown its rider. The horse has a saddle of Roman type with four pommels. The fallen rider must be a Celt for Romans did not show their countrymen being killed on their triumphal monuments.

Stirrups and spurs

Stirrups were not in general use in the ancient world. Their introduction transformed heavy cavalry and made possible the massively-armoured horsemen of mediaeval times. A primitive stirrup seems to have evolved in southern Russia during the early years of the Roman Empire and the *cataphractus* probably used some form of stirrup. Spurs were in use throughout the period.

Horseshoes

The traditional nailed-on horseshoe was in use from late Celtic times and was adopted by the Romans. However, a detachable horseshoe known as a hippo sandal was also in use. The latter was strapped to the horse's hoof.

It is difficult to know what its purpose was. Too many of them have survived for us to accept the opinion that they were for use by horses which had diseased hooves. Some, such as the one from Cambodunum in Germany, had studs and were therefore obviously for use on soft or muddy ground. However, it would have been almost impossible for the horse to gallop without throwing off a detachable shoe.

Bits

Horse bits had been in use in Italy and Greece since the Bronze Age and were nearly always of the snaffle type, made in two pieces.

Above: 2nd century cavalry helmet from Germany.
Below: 3rd century cataphractus armour from Dura Europos in Syria. Made of bronze scales sewn to a fabric and leather base, it fitted over the horse's back like a saddle blanket. The hole in the middle was for the saddle.

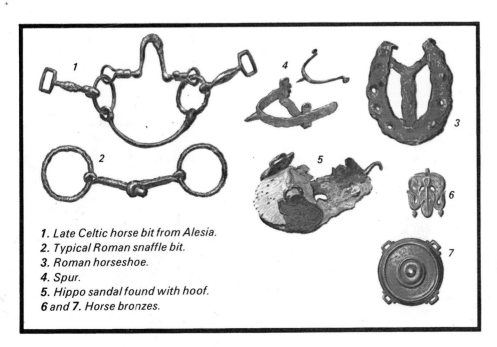

1. Late Celtic horse bit from Alesia.
2. Typical Roman snaffle bit.
3. Roman horseshoe.
4. Spur.
5. Hippo sandal found with hoof.
6 and 7. Horse bronzes.

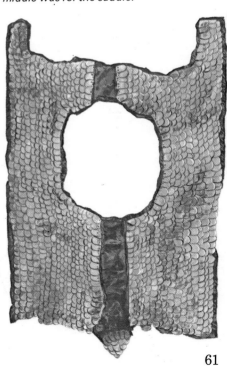

61

Siege Tactics and Equipment

Primus's troops sack Cremona

The Danube legions pursued the Vitellians as they fled for Cremona and immediately assaulted their camp. They rushed up to the ramparts, raising their shields in tortoise formation. They clambered across the ditch and up the turf mound and tried to pull down the palisade. The defenders deluged them with missiles from above but none broke through the wall of shields.

The catapults had been placed along the rampart, as was normal in camps. Now in desperation some of the Vitellian soldiers cut a large catapult loose from

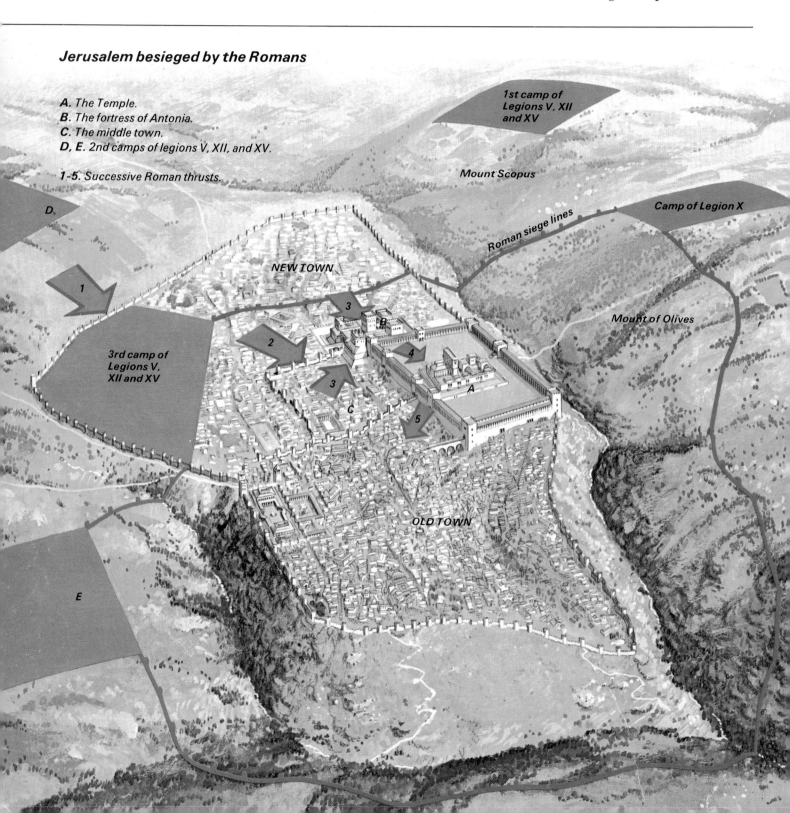

Jerusalem besieged by the Romans

A. The Temple.
B. The fortress of Antonia.
C. The middle town.
D, E. 2nd camps of legions V, XII, and XV.

1–5. Successive Roman thrusts.

D.

1st camp of Legions V, XII and XV

Mount Scopus

Camp of Legion X

Roman siege lines

NEW TOWN

3rd camp of Legions V, XII and XV

Mount of Olives

B

1

2

3

3

4

A

C

5

E

OLD TOWN

its moorings, heaved it over the palisade and down onto the legionaries' shields. Although the tortoise was crushed, the enormous weight of the machine brought down the palisade with it. The legionaries, climbing over the mangled bodies of their comrades, broke into the camp and drove all before them.

Their blood lust raised, the soldiers now assaulted the town which was full of visitors who had come in for the annual fair. Primus could do nothing to restrain them. They sacked the town for four days, and then burnt it to the ground, a pitiful end to the first military colony to be established beyond the Po. It had only been involved in the war because of its strategic position.

While these horrors were taking place in Italy, Titus, the son of Vespasian, marched on Jerusalem with legions *V Macedonia*, *X Fretensis*, *XII Fulminata* and *XV Apollinaris*.

The remnants of the Jewish forces had fled to the city and when the Romans arrived Jerusalem was bristling with defenders. Titus camped with Legions V, XII and XV on Mount Scopus to the north-east of the city while Legion X encamped on the Mount of Olives to the east.

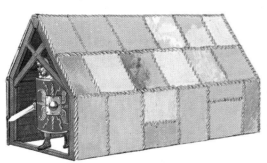

Above: *A hide-covered gallery as described by Vegetius; 5 metres long, 2½ metres high and just over 2 metres wide.*

Right: *27 legionaries in tortoise formation. The four ranks are shown by different colours.*

Below: *An iron-clad siege tower with drawbridge for mounting walls.*

Assault

The Romans used two methods to capture a fortified position: blockade (see page 32) and assault. For an assault, the catapults set up a barrage of stones and arrows to drive the defenders from the walls. Under cover of this barrage the legionaries would move up the rams and towers.

The Romans inherited their siege equipment from the Greeks. There are two main types: that used to protect the attackers as they approached the walls (screens, galleries and towers) and that used to assault the defenders (catapults and rams; see pages 66-67). Our main source for all these machines is Vitruvius, a Greek engineer.

Screens and galleries

Screens (*plutei*) protected the legionaries whilst they worked. They were probably made of wicker covered with hide. Galleries (*vineae*) were open-ended huts, sometimes on wheels, under which the legionaries could approach the walls. They were usually covered with untreated hide to protect them from fire. Galleries could be joined together to form a covered way from a position out of the enemy's range to the siege works or the walls themselves.

Towers

Towers were used to raise the besiegers to the level of the battlements. These towers were constructed of wood and covered with hides or metal plates to protect them from fire. They could be moved up to the walls either on wheels or rollers. These towers had floors at every three metres with ladders to take the soldiers from level to level.

Towers often exceeded 30 metres in height and could have balconies on the outside at various floor levels.

Tortoises

The name tortoise (*testudo*) was given to all moving armoured units, both machines and troop formations. The legionaries used a *testudo* to approach walls or ramparts (see above).

Above 27 men are shown formed up in four rows. The front row of six crouch down behind the shields of the middle four men which are held rim to rim. The two end men turn their shields outwards. The second, third and fourth rows of seven men each close up behind in a similar way, but the middle five men in each rank hold their shields above their heads. There are stories of chariots being run across these formations to test their strength.

Parades and Sports

Titus's attack on Jerusalem

So many internal conflicts raged in Jerusalem that there was hardly time to fight the Romans. Groups of religious fanatics had entered the city and were fighting each other to determine how the war should be waged. During these quarrels parts of the city were burned. The flames engulfed the granaries and vast hoards of food were destroyed. Only when Titus began his assault was any attempt made to unite the Jewish forces.

Jerusalem was composed of four parts, each with its own wall. The old town was built on a spur with

Parades

"As was their custom, the troops took their arms from the cases in which they had been stored up till now and advanced clad in mail to be paid. The cavalry led their horses which were richly caparisoned ... the scene glittered far and wide with silver and gold." This is how Josephus described Titus's pay parade which lasted four days; probably one day for each legion.

Josephus implies that the Romans had a special parade armour. If this was so very little of it remains today. Many face-covering helmets were once considered to be parade armour but are now known to be cavalry sports equipment. However, the elaborate helmet on the right, if it was ever worn, could only have been used for parades. Incidentally, it is the latest surviving example of the Etrusco-Corinthian type.

Pieces of 3rd century AD body armour (right) have survived. These are probably cavalry parade armour but might also have been worn for sports. Most legionary helmets had crest holders; yet crests were no longer worn in battle. Perhaps these helmets with crests were worn for parades.

Right: Part of the chest piece of a scale shirt from Yugoslavia.

Below: A gilded parade helmet from France.

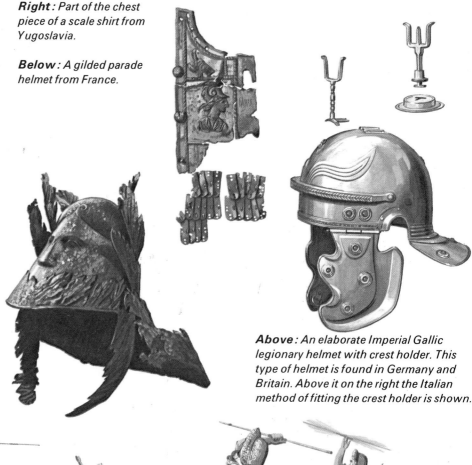

Above: An elaborate Imperial Gallic legionary helmet with crest holder. This type of helmet is found in Germany and Britain. Above it on the right the Italian method of fitting the crest holder is shown.

The hippica gymnasia. *One team acted as targets, the others charged in throwing light dummy javelins. Points were scored for hits. Scythian standards with long snakelike tails added colour.*

steep cliffs to the east, south and west. To the north of the old town was the massively-walled temple enclosure. Adjoining both the Temple and the old town was the middle town. The new town sprawled to the north-west.

Titus moved the camp of Legions V, XII and XV up to the walls of the new town and attacked. Due mainly to more squabbles among the defenders, it soon fell. Titus moved his main camp within the walls. Five days later, the middle town also fell.

Titus now divided his forces. He ordered two legions to attack the old city and two to attack the Temple. At the point where the middle town wall joined the Temple, Herod the Great had erected a fortress which he named Antonia in honour of his benefactor Mark Antony. At first the Romans tried to construct earthworks in order to get the siege machines up to the level of this fortress but the defenders undermined them and they collapsed.

Titus realized that the siege was likely to be long drawn out. He called a halt to give the defenders an opportunity to come to terms. His soldiers' pay was due and they paraded in front of the city to receive their four-monthly salary.

Cavalry sports

The cavalry sports (*hippica gymnasia*) were highly-skilled and colourful exhibitions performed by the cavalry using dummy javelins. These exhibitions were not unlike the mediaeval tournaments; both horse and man were elaborately armoured. Much cavalry sports equipment survives from all over the Empire.

The greatest find of this type comes from a 3rd century site at Straubing in Bavaria. This site has produced several helmets, greaves and horse face-pieces in a remarkable state of preservation. Helmets which have been found as far afield as Britain (Ribchester) and Israel (Hebron) come in male and female types suggesting perhaps that the contestants represented Greeks and Amazons.

Above: 1st century sports equipment.
1. Bronze helmet from Bulgaria.
2. Leather chamfron and eyepiece from northern Britain. **3**. Bronze horse eyeguards from Pompeii.

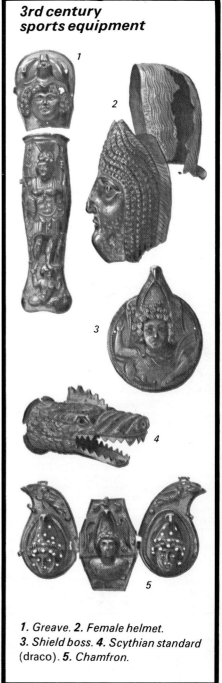

3rd century sports equipment

1. Greave. **2**. Female helmet.
3. Shield boss. **4**. Scythian standard (draco). **5**. Chamfron.

Siege Weapons: Rams and Catapults

Jerusalem refuses to surrender

When the Jews still refused to surrender, Titus threw up a rampart and palisade around the city, as Caesar had done at Alesia, in order that none might escape. Having secured the whole circuit of the city, Titus re-erected the earthworks against the Fortress of Antonia. These earthworks were faced with timber.

The defenders of the fortress sallied from the gates, attacked the guards and tried to fire the timbers. But the legionaries were ready for them and beat them back. The battering rams were now brought to bear on the walls. The soldiers advanced

Above: A battering ram as described by Vitruvius. The beam was a squared-off timber tapering towards the head. The end was plated with iron and capped with an iron head in the shape of a ram. The timber was bound with rope and then covered with raw hides.

Right: A tortoise ram based on Vitruvius. The housing was of heavy timbers covered with thick planking surmounted by a layer of green wicker to break the force of stones.

As a fire precaution the whole housing was covered with fresh seaweed sandwiched between two layers of untreated hide.

Rams

The battering ram was merely a development of the primitive method of assaulting fortifications where a tree trunk was used to knock a hole through a wall. The Assyrians, followed by the Persians and Greeks, developed complex machines to perform this task.

The Romans copied their predecessors. Their machines consisted of a housing built of sturdy timbers rather like a hut on wheels. This protected the soldiers operating the machine. The ram was placed inside suspended by ropes. It had an iron head, sometimes in the form of a ram's head. The beam was bound with ropes, both lengthways and around, to stop it splitting.

The housings of Roman siege machines were covered with raw hides or metal plates. Rams were also often built into siege towers.

Catapults

Catapults were a Greek invention and came in two types: stone throwing (*ballista*) and arrow shooting (*catapulta*). These machines resembled outsize crossbows except that the power was supplied not by the bow but by springs of twisted sinew. The single armed stone-thrower (*onager*) did not come into use until the late Empire.

The size varied from small arrow-shooters, about 2 metres high, to vast machines capable of throwing stones weighing more than 45 kilos. Stones used in the Jewish war have been found, some as small as oranges and others, including one from the ruins of the Antonia Fortress, weighing over 45 kilos.

Only the legions used artillery. Each legion had about 60 catapults, including the lighter types and the very heavy stone throwers.

Painted stones

Josephus tells how, during the siege of Jerusalem, the Jews on the walls could see the larger stones coming as they were light in colour and stood out against the dark background.

The Romans realized this and therefore painted the stones dark. This is interesting as it suggests that these machines did not "lob" the stones but shot them in a low trajectory.

Josephus also takes great delight in telling how a man's head was knocked off and carried "three furlongs" by a *ballista* stone.

Uses of artillery

Although catapults were used mainly in sieges, both for defence and attack, we find Caesar using the lighter catapults on the open battlefield. Catapults were regularly used in sea warfare as well.

in tortoise formation and, under the protection of their shields, hacked away at the foundations of the fortress.

That night the wall collapsed as a result of the constant battering and of the network of tunnels that the defenders had driven under their own fortifications in an attempt to undermine the earthworks. Foreseeing this possibility, the defenders had erected another wall on the inside. The legionaries struggled in vain to take this wall for two days. They could neither assault it nor could they bring their rams to bear on it. Then, on the second night, a small party of legionaries, including trumpeters, scaled the walls under cover of darkness and killed the sentries. They sounded their trumpets and Titus led his forces to assault the wall.

The defenders believed that the fortress had been taken, left their posts and retreated to the Temple. Titus then destroyed most of the fortress so that he could push a ramp straight up through to the Temple platform and bring up the towers and rams. Famine had forced the defenders to discontinue the daily sacrifice; even so the Temple held out for another five weeks.

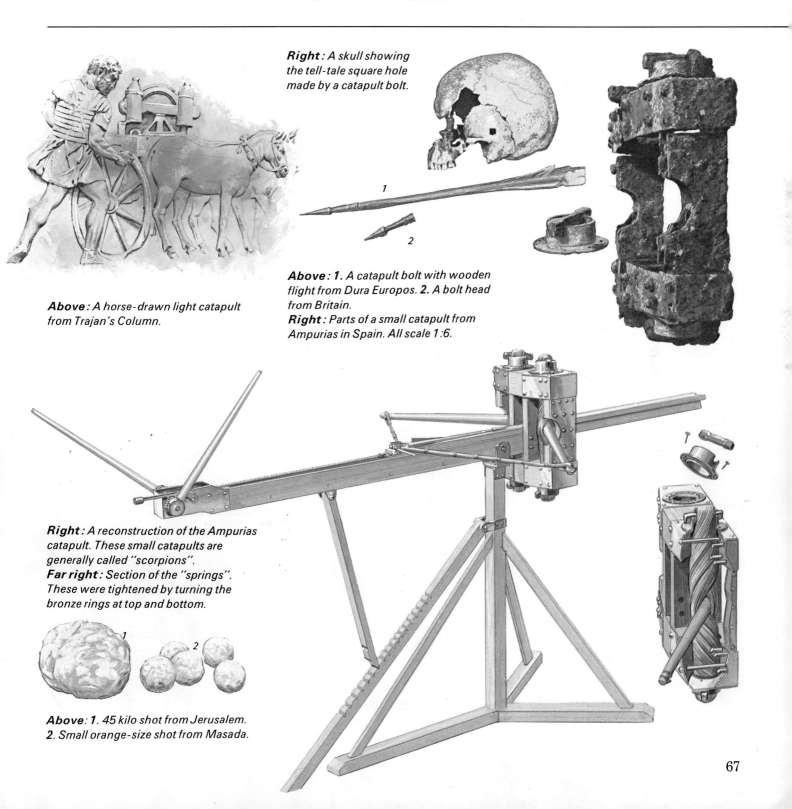

Above: A horse-drawn light catapult from Trajan's Column.

Right: A skull showing the tell-tale square hole made by a catapult bolt.

Above: 1. A catapult bolt with wooden flight from Dura Europos. 2. A bolt head from Britain.
Right: Parts of a small catapult from Ampurias in Spain. All scale 1:6.

Right: A reconstruction of the Ampurias catapult. These small catapults are generally called "scorpions".
Far right: Section of the "springs". These were tightened by turning the bronze rings at top and bottom.

Above: 1. 45 kilo shot from Jerusalem.
2. Small orange-size shot from Masada.

Rewards and Punishments

The fall of Jerusalem

Titus tried to spare the Temple at Jerusalem. All attempts to obtain a surrender failed, however, and the battering rams proved fruitless. In desperation, Titus gave orders for the gates of the Temple enclosure to be fired.

The flames soon spread to the porticoes but, in their fury, the Jews did little to quench them. Much of the outer enclosure was destroyed. Two days later, after severe fighting around the outer court of the Temple, the Romans burst into the inner court. A Roman soldier threw a firebrand into the Temple.

Above: Tombstone of the centurion M Caelius showing his decorations: oak leaf crown, phalerae, armillae *and* torques.

Above: A set of phalerae *from Germany. They are made of silver with gold inlay.*

Above: A tombstone from Dalmatia showing phalerae, armillae *and* torques *on a harness.*

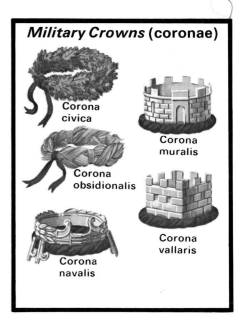

Military Crowns (coronae)

Corona civica
Corona muralis
Corona obsidionalis
Corona vallaris
Corona navalis

Rewards

The Republican soldier was entitled to a share of the booty taken on campaign. There was less opportunity for this sort of reward under the Empire, so, in order to keep the troops happy, the emperors gave peace-time pay-outs (donatives).

Such a payment was made when a new emperor succeeded to the throne. This was often equivalent to five years' pay. The Praetorians were offered ten years' pay to put Galba on the throne.

There were also military decorations. During the Republic these were won largely on merit and regardless of rank. The most prized of these was the *corona obsidionalis*, a grass crown given to the deliverer of a besieged army. Pliny, writing in the 1st century AD, only names eight people who had received it.

The *corona civica* was an oak leaf crown awarded to a soldier who saved the life of a fellow citizen. There were also two gold crowns; the *corona muralis*, awarded to the first man over the wall in a siege, and the *corona vallaris* for the first man over

the rampart during a siege.

After the fall of Cartagena in Spain, Scipio awarded a *corona muralis* to a legionary centurion and a marine. There was also the *corona navalis*, which was awarded for the capture of an enemy ship. This could only be won by a Consul.

During the Empire decorations were restricted to various ranks. Nobody below the rank of centurion could win the *corona muralis* or *vallaris*. However, common soldiers could be awarded large medals (*phalerae*), arm bands (*armillae*) and neck bands (torques). A centurion usually received these as well as the gold crowns.

First centurions and junior tribunes could also receive a silver spear (*hasta pura*). There was also a plain gold crown (*corona aurea*) which could be awarded to centurions and above. Senior tribunes might expect two gold crowns, two silver spears and also two small gold standards (*vexilla*). Legionary legates could receive three each of these and provincial governors of consular rank, four.

The furniture and drapes in the shrine caught fire and the whole building was reduced to ashes.

Simon bar Giora, who had commanded the defence of the Temple, escaped to the old town. He was captured there a month later when that part finally fell. The old town had experienced all the rigours of starvation. In the last days mothers were said to have eaten their own children.

The city was turned over to the soldiers. When they had wearied of their killing and pillaging it was set on fire. Titus then ordered the remains to be levelled to the ground leaving only three of the highest towers and part of the wall standing. The wall was for the encampment of the garrison and the towers to remind people of the grandeur of the city that had once stood there.

Josephus suggests that over a million Jews perished in the siege. This figure is obviously an enormous exaggeration, for a city of this size could not have supported that number of people during a six-month siege.

Titus now assembled his troops, to reward the valiant and to punish the cowardly, as was the custom after a battle.

Right: Fustuarium. *The punishment of sentries who desert their posts.*

Below: *The* aquilifer *Cnaeus Musius of Legion XIV Gemina, wearing his decorations.*

Punishments
Roman military discipline was severe though not so severe as many ancient authors would pretend. The Roman army had a great tradition of discipline.

We read of generals executing their own sons for disobedience. We also hear occasionally of whole legions being banished.

The latter happened to the remnants of the army that was defeated by Hannibal at the Battle of Cannae. The defeated legions were banished from Italy for the duration of the war and did not return to their own homes for 14 years. However, these sorts of things were isolated incidents and were not general practice.

Capital punishment
Capital punishment was occasionally used. It usually meant being beaten or stoned to death (*fustuarium*). This was the punishment given to deserters and to sentries who left their posts. It was carried out by the comrades whose lives had been put at risk.

Decimation
If a whole unit deserted in battle, or mutinied, the death penalty was sometimes inflicted in the form known as "decimation".

For this punishment, one in every ten men would be selected by lot to be executed. The remainder were disgraced and would be forced to live on barley instead of their normal corn ration. They might also be made to live outside the defences of the camp.

Lesser punishments
These extreme punishments were unusual. More often soldiers were given lesser punishments. These included caning, extra duties, reduction in rank or dishonourable discharge.

Disbandment
The greatest dishonour that could happen to a whole unit was disbandment. This was to happen to four of the mutinous German legions when Vespasian came to the throne.

Triumph and Ovation

Vespasian wins the contest

After their victory at Cremona, the Danubian legions marched on Rome. In the city the supporters of Vitellius fought desperately. The crowds lined the roofs, urging the victors on, and climbing down to rob the dead. Vitellius had hidden in the palace. He was found by the soldiers and dragged to the Forum where he was killed amid the jeers of the mob. The Danubian legions were now completely out of control and pillaged the city unchecked until the arrival of Mucianus a month later.

The revolt which had broken out in Germany was

Left: A relief from Rome showing a trophy and prisoners to be carried shoulder high by eight legionaries.

Below: A relief from the triumphal arch of Titus showing the treasure from the temple at Jerusalem being carried in triumph.

Origins of the Triumph

According to the famous legend, the first Romans had no women and so they kidnapped some from the local villages. In the battle that followed, Romulus, the Roman king, killed the leader of the villagers in single combat.

Stripping the dead chieftain of his armour, Romulus hung it over an oak branch to form a trophy. Then, crowned with a laurel wreath, he raised this trophy onto his shoulder and led his men in procession singing songs of triumph. This was the origin of the victory celebration which was to resound through the pages of history under the name of the Triumph.

now in full swing. Several Gallic tribes were encouraged by the civil disturbances in the Empire and had joined forces with the Germans to declare a Gallic Empire. The depleted legions along the Rhine were attacked and their camps burned. The disorder which had infected these legions for so long now reached its climax.

The troops (Legion *XVI Gallica*) based at Neuss killed the provincial governor, put their officers in chains and swore allegiance to the Gallic Empire. Never in the history of Rome had the army sunk to such a level. The Rhine frontier from Mainz to the coast was now in enemy hands and a complete legion had been massacred. But the rebels had over-estimated the effects of the civil war and were soon to find themselves opposed by massive Roman armies from the south.

The Gallic Empire collapsed within a year of its birth. Vespasian clamped down ruthlessly on the German legions. Four were disbanded in disgrace and one was transferred to the Danube.

Now installed as Emperor, Vespasian awaited the arrival of Titus from Judaea so that they could celebrate his Triumph together.

The procession

As Rome's conquests grew, the triumph evolved in complexity and splendour. Although it varied from general to general, a format developed.

At the head of the procession came the magistrates and the senators. Behind these the booty which had been taken from the enemy was carried with paintings or models of the battles and the captured cities. White oxen followed for the sacrifice.

Then came the prisoners, sometimes carried shoulder high on platforms with trophies of armour. Behind the prisoners the general rode in a gilded chariot drawn by four horses. The general's face was painted red and he was clothed like a king. In his hands he carried a sceptre and an olive branch. Behind him in the chariot rode a slave who whispered "remember you are just a man".

Behind the chariot came the soldiers wearing laurel wreaths and shouting "*Io Triomphe*" (behold the Triumph). It was traditional for the soldiers to sing bawdy songs, for on this day the general could hardly punish them.

The route

The procession wound through the streets of Rome. It passed through the two circuses before coming round the Palatine Hill and up the sacred way to the Forum. Here the chief prisoner was led off to execution. Both Vercingetorix and Simon bar Giora suffered this fate. Perseus, being a king, was spared and ended his days in prison.

The procession climbed the Capitoline Hill and waited for news of the prisoner's execution. Then the general sacrificed the white oxen outside the Temple of Jupiter.

The ovation

Only a general who had won a complete victory over a foreign enemy could Triumph. During the Empire this was restricted to the Emperor and his family.

There was, however, a lesser form called an ovation. The general sacrificed on the Alban Mount several kilometres south of the city. He entered Rome either on horseback or on foot the following morning. Instead of a laurel wreath he wore a crown of myrtle.

Above: *The relief from a silver cup found at Boscoreale in Italy. It shows the* triumphator *in his chariot (left) and sacrificing an ox to Jupiter on the Capitol (right).*

Above: *The triumphal arch of Titus.*

The Triumph
of Titus

The Triumph of Titus nears its end. The procession has passed through the Forum and is now climbing the steep hill to the Capitol. It was at this point that Simon bar Giora was dragged off to execution.

73

Glossary

The plural form is given after the Latin nouns.

agger the mound of earth used for defence works.

aia, alae cavalry regiment (literally a wing).

aquila, aquilae the eagle—the legion standard.

aquilifer the eagle bearer.

armilla, armillae arm band—a military decoration.

Attic helmet a Greek helmet popular in Athens.

augur one who examines natural happenings to see whether God approves of a course of action.

auxiliaries soldiers other than legionaries who served with the Roman army.

baldric shoulder strap for carrying sword.

ballista, ballistae stone-throwing machine.

bas-relief flat sculpture with figures raised only slightly from the background.

bireme a galley with two banks of oars.

boss the raised centre portion of a shield.

butt the foot of a spear or javelin.

caliga, caligae a military sandal.

caltrop metal spike thrown on the ground to hinder cavalry and infantry.

cataphractus heavily-armed cavalryman

catapulta, catapultae arrow-shooting machine.

centuria, centuriae an area about 700 metres square.

centurions the professional commissioned officers of the Roman army.

century a unit of soldiers usually about 80 strong.

chamfron face armour for a horse.

cohors equitata, cohortes equitatae units of mixed cavalry and infantry.

cohort one tenth of a legion or a unit of between 500 and 1000 strong.

consul chief Roman magistrate. There were two for each year.

corduroy logs laid side by side.

cornicen, cornicines a military horn blower.

cornu a military horn.

corona, coronae a crown.

corvus raven—the nickname given to the boarding plank.

cuirass body armour.

decurion cavalry officer.

diploma, diplomae a certificate of Roman citizenship.

dolabra, dolabrae military pick-axe.

donative cash payment to the army.

dowel a wooden rod.

draco a standard in the form of a dragon.

eques, equites horseman—pl. cavalry.

Etrusco-Corinthian helmet a debased form of the Greek face-covering helmet.

extraordinarii a section of the Roman army which guarded the consul in Republican times.

ferrule a metal band holding a javelin head to the wooden shaft.

forum market place.

fossa, fossae ditch.

frumentarius, frumentarii intelligence officer.

galley a warship propelled by oars.

genius, genii a spirit which unites groups of people.

gladius, gladii a short sword.

gladius hispaniensis the legionary's sword.

graffito, graffiti picture scratched on stone.

greave a leg guard.

groma, gromae a surveying instrument.

gunwale the fence-like structure along the edge of a ship's deck.

hasta pura silver spear—a military decoration.

hastatus, hastati the front rank of the legion. Also a centurion of the first cohort.

hastatus posterior the rear centurion of a *hastatus* maniple.

hastatus prior front centurion of a *hastatus* maniple.

Hellenistic objects produced under the influence of Greek culture between about 300 and 50 BC.

hippica gymnasia cavalry sports.

hippo sandal a detachable horseshoe.

imago standard bearing the Emperor's image.

Imperial Gallic helmet a type of Roman helmet derived from a Gallic prototype.

"Jockey Cap" a type of helmet characterized by a large back peak.

legatus, legati commanders of legions and provincial governors.

legion a brigade of between 4000 and 6000 Roman citizen soldiers.

lictor a body guard to the consul.

"lilies" round holes with pointed stakes in them.

magistrates (Republican) the name given to the annually-elected chief political/military officers.

magistrates (Imperial) senior political officers nominated by the Emperor annually.

maniple two centuries coupled together.

marine a soldier who served with the fleet.

milliary 1000 strong.

montage group of pictures made up into one.

Montefortino helmet a type of Celtic helmet adopted by the Romans in the 4th century BC.

mortice method of joining two pieces of wood with a flat tongue.

nock the notch for attaching the string to the ends of a bow.

onager single-armed stone throwing machine.

optio, optiones a centurion's second-in-command.

outrigger an extension beyond the sides of a galley to give the oars greater leverage.

ovation a lesser form of Triumph.

palisade a wooden fence built for defence.

parma equestris the round cavalry shield used during the Republic.

phalanx military formation in which the soldiers fight shoulder to shoulder.

phalera, phalerae large military medals.

"pig's head" "spear head" military formation.

pilum, pila the heavy javelin of the legionaries.

pilus, pili an alternative form of *triarius*.

pilus posterior the rear centurion of a *triarius* maniple.

pilus prior front centurion of a *triarius* maniple.

pluteus, plutei screen used to protect soldiers while working.

praefectus, praefecti prefect. Commander of an auxiliary or allied battalion.

praefectus castrorum camp prefect.

praefectus praetorio commander of the Praetorian guard.

praefectus urbanus commander of the urban cohorts.

praefectus vigilum commander of the *Vigiles*.

Praetorian Guard the Emperor's bodyguard.

praetorium the area of the camp where the commander lived.

primi ordines centurions of the first cohort.

primus pilus the first centurion of the legion.

princeps, principes 2nd rank of the legion; also a centurion of the first cohort.

princeps posterior the rear centurion of a *principes* maniple.

princeps prior front centurion of a *principes* maniple.

principalis, principales officer below the rank of centurion.

principia headquarters building in a camp.

pteriges strips of leather or fabric for protection of thighs and shoulders.

quadrireme a galley with four banks of oars.

quaestionarius, quaestionarii torturer or interrogator.

quaestor junior magistrate.

quaestorium the area of the camp in Republican times where the *quaestor* had his office.

quinquereme a galley with five banks of of oars.

"raven" the naval boarding plank.

"scorpion" a small catapult.

scutum, scuta the legionary shield.
Senate the Roman parliament.
signum, signa the century standard.
signifer the century standard bearer.
spatha, spathae the long cavalry
sword.
speculator, speculatores a military
executioner.
sprit sail the small square sail at the
front of a vessel.
stock (lead) cross bar of an anchor.
tang the part of a weapon blade that fits
into the handle.
tessera, tesserae the small plaque with
the password written on it.
tesserarius, tesserarii the guard
commander.
testudo, testudines tortoise formation
or an armoured siege machine.
torques neck bands—military
decorations.
"tortoise" see *testudo*.
triarius, triarii third rank of the legion.
tribunes senior officers who served
under the legion commander.
tribunus angusticlavius junior tribune.
tribunus laticlavius senior tribune.
trierarch captain of a galley.
trireme galley with three banks of oars.
Triumph victory procession.
tubicen, tubicines trumpeter.
turma, turmae cavalry unit.
urban cohorts the city guard.
vanguard the front of a marching army.
veles, velites light armed legionary of
the Republic.
vexillum, vexilla a flag used by cohorts
and legionary detachments.
via praetoria the road running from
front to rear of camp.
via principalis the road running from
side to side of camp.
via quintana a secondary camp road
running parallel to *via principalis*.
vigil, vigiles city night policeman/
fireman.
vinea, vineae covered gallery used in
siege operations.

People

Agricola (AD 40-90) Governor of
Britain.
Alexander the Great (356-323 BC) the
king of Macedonia who conquered Persia.
Augustus (63 BC-AD 14) first Roman
Emperor. The date at which his reign
began is complicated. He had complete
control from 31 BC.
Caesar, Julius (c.100-44 BC) the
Roman general who conquered Gaul and
overthrew the Roman Republic.
Celts the main barbarian occupants of
Western Europe.
Cleopatra Queen of Egypt (d. 31 BC).
Commodus Roman Emperor
(AD 176-192).

Constantine Roman Emperor
(AD 306-337).
Domitian Roman Emperor (AD 81-96).
Fabricius (1st century BC) Roman
famous for building the bridge that bears
his name.
Galba Emperor for 4 months (AD 68-69).
Gauls the occupants of N.W. Europe,
west of the Rhine.
Hadrian Emperor (AD 117-138)
organized Rome's frontier defences.
Hannibal (247-182 BC) Carthaginian
general.
Helvetii the ancient occupants of
Switzerland.
Josephus (1st century AD) Jewish
historian.
Lucullus (1st century BC) Roman
general who invaded Armenia.
Marius (157-86 BC) Roman general
who reformed the army.
Mark Antony (82-30 BC) colleague of
Caesar. Later allied himself to Cleopatra
and committed suicide with her after
defeat at Actium.
Mucianus (1st century AD) Vespasian's
lieutenant in charge of the invasion of
Italy.
Nero Roman Emperor (AD 54-68).
Otho Roman Emperor for 4 months
(AD 69).
Paullus, Aemilius (3rd-2nd century BC)
Roman general who conquered Macedon.
Polybius (2nd century BC) Greek
historian.
Pompey (106-48 BC) Roman general
who conquered Syria and Palestine.
Primus, Antonius (1st century AD)
Legionary commander who invaded Italy
on behalf of Vespasian.
Romulus legendary first king of Rome.
Scipio (236-184 BC) Roman general
who defeated Hannibal.
Scipio Aemilianus (185-129 BC)
Roman general who reduced Numantia.
Simon bar Giora (1st century AD) a
leader of the Jewish revolt.
Tacitus (1st-2nd century AD) Roman
historian.
Tiberius Emperor (AD 14-37) the
successor of Augustus.
Titus Emperor (AD 79-81) the general
who destroyed Jerusalem.
Trajan Emperor (AD 98-117)
Conquered Dacia and Mesopotamia.
Valens (1st century AD) commander of
Vitellius's forces.
Vegetius (4th century AD) Roman
writer.
Vercingetorix (1st century BC) leader
of Gallic revolt against Caesar.
Verginius (1st century AD) commander
of the army of northern Germany.
Vespasian general sent by Nero to put
down the Jewish revolt. Roman
Emperor (AD 69-79).
Vindex (1st century AD) Governor of
the Lyons area of France.
Vitellius Emperor (AD 69)
Vitruvius (1st century BC) Roman
architect and engineer.

Places and Battles

Actium town on west coast of Greece.
Actium, Battle of (31 BC), sea battle.
Augustus defeated Antony and Cleopatra.
Alesia town in central France.
Alesia, Siege of (52 BC), the siege that
marked the final conquest of Gaul.
Algerian War (111-105 BC)
(Jugurthine War) fought by Rome against
the nomads of Algeria.
Avaricum, Siege of (52 BC), town in
Gaul stormed by Caesar.
Cannae, Battle of (216 BC), Hannibal's
greatest victory in which 60,000 Romans
were said to have been killed.
Capitol the citadel at Rome.
Capua, Siege of (211 BC). Capua joined
Hannibal after Battle of Cannae and was
retaken by the Romans five years later.
Carthage just north of Tunis in North
Africa. Main rival of Rome in west
Mediterranean. Home of Hannibal.
Carthaginian Wars wars fought
between Rome and Carthage. 1st,
264-241 BC; 2nd, 218-201 BC;
3rd, 149-146 BC.
Cynoscephalae, Battle of (197 BC),
final battle of Rome's 2nd war with
Macedon.
Dacia area north of Danube, roughly
Romania/Hungary.
Etruria Tuscany—the area north of
Rome.
Etruscan Wars the wars fought between
Rome and Etruria in the 5th-3rd
centuries BC.
Gallic Empire a breakaway empire
formed by the Gauls and Germans in
AD 70.
Gallic Wars the wars between Rome and
the Gauls in the 4th-1st centuries BC.
Jerusalem, Siege of (AD 70), the
attempt of the Jews to throw off the
Roman yoke.
Macedonia (Macedon) the area north of
Greece roughly equivalent to southern
Yugoslavia.
Macedonian Wars the three wars fought
between Rome and Macedon between
213 and 168 BC.
Numantia town in northern Spain
besieged by the Romans in 133 BC.
Olympus mountain in north-east Greece;
the home of the Gods.
Palatine Hill the hill in Rome on which
the royal palaces were built.
Phoenicia roughly equivalent to
Lebanon.
Pompeii a town near Naples destroyed
when Vesuvius erupted in AD 79.
Pydna, Battle of (168 BC), battle in
which Macedon was defeated.
Sacred island the island in the Tiber.
Syracuse, Siege of (211 BC), Greek port
in Sicily besieged by the Romans during
the war with Hannibal.
Zama, Battle of (202 BC), Hannibal
defeated by Scipio.

Index

Numbers in bold refer to
illustrations

Actium, battle of, 21
Aemilianus, Scipio, 9, 42
agger, see camp, defences of
Alesia, excavations at, 35
Alesia, siege of, **24-25**, 31, 32-33, **32-33**, 66
allies, 11, 12, 16, 27
Alps, roads over, 30, **30**
Ampurias, catapult from, **67**
anchor, **22**
Antonia fortress, **36-37**, **62**, 65, 66-67
Antony, Mark, 20, 21, 65
aprons, legionary, 50, **51**
aquila, 44, 45, **45**, 47, **47**, 52, **69**
archers, Cretan, 54
    eastern, **54**, 55
    mounted, 59
    naval, 23
armillae, 68, **68**
armour, auxiliary, 55, **55**
    Caesarian, 26, 34-35, **34-35**
    cavalry, 60-61, **60-61**, 64-65, **64-65**
    centurion's, 46, **46**
    horse, 59, 65, **65**
    imperial, 48-49, **48-49**, 50, **50**
    officer's, 34, **35**
    parade, 64, **64**
    republican, 18-19, **18-19**
arrows, 55, **55**
artillery, 66-67, **67**
Augustus, 20, 21, 38, 42, 56, 58
Aurelius Victorinus, helmet of, **43**
auxiliaries, 38, 41, 52, 53, 54-55, **54-55**
Avaricum, siege of, 30-31, **31**

baggage, 12, 27, 53, **53**
baldric, 50, **51**
ballista stones, 66, **67**
banishment, 69
barrack blocks, 15, **15**, 38, 39, **39**
baths, 45
battle array, 16-17, **16-17**
battle tactics, 16-17
beak of ship, 20, **20**, 23
Bedriacum, battle at, 47
Belgium, conquest of, 27
belts, 50, **51**
bireme, 22
blockades, 32-33
boarding plank, 20, **21**
bolt, catapult, **67**
booty, 31, 68, 71

Boscoreale, cup from, 70-71
bow, composite, 55, **55**
box rampart, **39**
breast plates, 18
Brenner Pass, 55
bridges, 28-29, **28-29**
Britain, 27, 37, 38
Britain, fleet of, 21
bucket, legionary, 53, **53**

Caelius M, tombstone of, **68**
Caesar, Julius, 17, 20, 24-35, 38, 41, 58, 66
caliga, 50, **50**
caltrop, 33
camp, breaking of, 12, 52, **53**
    cavalry, 33
    defences of, 12-13, **13**, 14-15, **14-15**, 32-33, 39, **39**
    gates of, 14-15, **14-15**, 39
    marching, 13, 14-15, **14-15**, 38
    permanent, 38-39, **39**
    pitching of, 12-13, **13**
    praetorian, 43
    site of, 12
    stone, 38-39, **39**
    timber, 38, **39**, **56**
Cancelleria, relief, **42**, **51**
Cannae, battle of, 17, 58, 69
Capitoline Hill (Capitol), 10, 11, 71
Capua, 33
    centuriation at, 56, **56**
Carthage, 20, 23
cataphractus, 60, 61
    armour, **61**
catapults, 23, 62, 63, 66, **67**
cavalry, 10, 11, 12, 14, 16, 33, 54, 56, 58-59, **58-59**, 60-61, **60-61**
    Gallic, 58
    German, 31, 45, 53, 58, 59
    Hannibal's, 58
    legionary, 41, **41**, 52
    light, 59, **59**
    Sarmatian, 58
    Spanish, 58
centuriation, 56, **56**
centurions, 11, 13, **13**, 16, 17, 31, **40**, 46, **46-47**, 68
century, 10, 16, 38
circumvallation, 31, 32-33, **32-33**, **62**, 66
citizenship, Roman, 21, 26, 27, 41, 55
civil wars, 38, 71
Cleopatra, 20
cohort, first, **40**, 41, 44, 47
cohorts, 26, **26**, 27, **40-41**, 41
cohorts, Praetorian, 42-43
Cohortes Equitatae, 59
    camp of, 56
colonies, 30, 56, 63
consuls, 10, 11, 12, 26, 42
Corbridge, armour from, 48, **48**
Corbulo M Spedius, diploma of, **55**
cornicen, 11, **11**, **40**, 47, **47**, 52, 67
cornu, 12, **12**, 16
coronae (crowns), 68, **68**
corvus, 20, **21**
Cremona, 47, 55, 56, 57, 59
    battle of, 47, 50, 52
    sack of, 62-63
cuirass, 18
    centurion's, 27, 46
    general's, 27
    muscled, 34, **35**
Cynoscephalae, battle of, 17
Dacia, 28
dagger, Roman, 35, **35**, 50, 51, **51**
    Spanish, 18, **19**

Danube, 38, 58, 59
    bridge over, 28, 29, **29**
    defences of, 57
    fleet on, 21
    road along, 30
decimation, 69
decorations, military, 68, **68**, **69**
decurion, 11, 58
defences, see camp
Delphi, Paullus monument at, 18, **18**, 34, 58, **58**
deserters, 14, 69
diet, 53
diploma, 55, **55**
disbandment, 69, 71
discharge, 26, 34, 55, 69
discipline, 17, 69
dispatch riders, 41, **41**
dolabra, **32**, 33
Domitian, 41, 42
Domitius Ahenobarbus, altar of, 34-35, **34-35**, 58, **58**
donatives, 43, 44, 68
drill, 44
Dubitatus, Junius, shield boss of, 50, **50**
Dura Europos, shields from, 50, **50**, **55**
    horse armour from, **61**
    catapult bolt from, **67**

earthworks, 31, **31**, 66
Egypt, fleet at, 21
    shield from, 18, **18**
engineering, military, 28-33
entrenching, 13, **13**
equipment, cavalry, 60-61, **60-61**
    legionary, 26, 38, 52-53, **52-53**
equites, 47
extraordinarii, 11, 12, 42
ferrules, *pilum*, **35**
fleet, 20-21
fort, auxiliary, 54, 55, 56, **56**, 57
fortress, legionary, 38, **39**, 56, 57
forum, of camp, 14, **14-15**, 39, **39**
Forum, Roman, 70, 71
fossa, see camp defences
frontiers, 38, 41, 58
    control of, 56, 57, **57**
frumentarii, 47
fustuarium, 14, 69, **69**

Galba, 41-47, 68
galleries, **31**, 63, **63**
galleys, 20-21, **21**, 22-23, **22-23**
Gaul, conquest of, 25-33
Genii, 45
Germany, 29, 38
    armies of, 41, 42, 44, 45
Germany, conquest of, see camp
Giora, Simon bar, 69, 71
Gladius Hispaniensis, 18, **19**
    see also sword, legionary
granaries, 39, **39**, **56**
Great St Bernard, road over, 30, **30**
greaves, 18, 34, 35
    centurion's, 46, **46**, **47**
    sports, 65
groma, 12, **12**
guard commanders, see *tesserarii*
guards, imperial, 42-43, **42-43**

Hadrian, 57
Hadrian, wall of, 57, **57**
Hannibal, 17, 30, 45, 69
    war with, 10, 23, 33, 56
hasta pura, 68
hastatus, 10, **10**, 12, 14-16, 26, 27, 46
helmets, attic, 19, **19**

auxiliary, 55, **55**
    Caesarian, 34, **35**
    cavalry, 60, **60**, **61**
    centurions', 46, **46**, **47**
    Etrusco-Corinthian, 19, **19**, 34, **35**, 49, 64, **64**
    Gallic, 49, **49**
    Hellenistic, 35, **35**
    Imperial, 43, 49, **49**
    Imperial Gallic, 49, **49**, 64
    Italian, 49, **49**
    Jockey Cap, 49, **49**
    Montefortino, 19, **19**, 34, **35**, 49, **49**
    Republican, 18-19, **19**
    sports, 65, **65**
Helvetii, 26-27
Herculaneum, helmet from, **43**
hippica gymnasia, 64-65, **64-65**
horse equipment, 60, **61**
hospitals, 38, **38**, **56**
Hostilia, 55, 56

imago, 44
infantry, 10, 26
    auxiliary, 54-55, **54**
intelligence officers, see *frumentarii*
Iron Gates, bridge at, 28, **29**

javelin of legionary, see *pilum*
javelin of *velites*, 10, 18-19, **19**
javelineers, naval, 23
Jerusalem, siege of, 31, **36-37**, 37, 46, **62**, 62-69
    ballista shot from, 66, **67**
Jewish revolt, 37, 38, 41, 46-47, 52
Josephus, 31, 37, 60, 66, 69

Kastell Künzing, fort at, **56**

Lacus Curtius, relief from, 58, **58**
Lake Nemi, ships from, **22**, 23, **23**
legate (*legatus*), 27, **40**, 46, 47, 52, 68
legionary, republican, 10, **10**, 17, 18
    Caesarian, 26, **26**, 29, 30, 31, 33, 34
    Imperial, **36-37**, 41, **44-45**
    professional, 26
legion I Germanica, 38
    I Italica, 38
    II Augusta, 38
    III Augusta, 38, 54
    III Cyrenaica, 38, 46
    III Gallica, 38
    IV Macedonica, 38
    IV Scythica, 38
    V Alaudae, 38, 45
    V Macedonica, 38, 62, 63, 65
    VI Ferrata, 38, 52
    VI Victrix, 38
    VII Claudia, 38
    VIII Augusta, 38, 50
    IX Hispana, 38
    X Fretensis, 38, 62, 63
    X Gemina, 38
    XI Claudia, 38
    XII Fulminata, 38, 62, 63, 65
    XIII Gemina, 38
    XIV Gemina, 38, 69
    XV Apollinaris, 38, 62, 63, 65
    XV Primigenia, 38, 69
    XVI Gallica, 38, 39, 71
    XX Valeria Victrix, 38, 46
    XXI Rapax, 38, 45
    XXII Deiotariana, 38
    XXII Primigenia, 38
legions, Augustan, 41

British, 38, 55
Caesarian, 20, 26-27, 30, 31
Danubian, 38, 45, 47, 52, 53, 55, 56, 62
Egyptian, 38, 47
German, 38, 42, 44, 45, 54, 55, 69, 71
Imperial, 38, 40-41, **40-41**
permanent, 26
position in camp, 14-15
Republican, 10, 11, **11**, 12, 16, 17
Syrian, 38, 47
levy, military, 10
lictors, 42, **42**
"lilies", 32, **32**

Macedon, 9-17
mail, 18-19, **19**, 26, 34, 55, **55**, 59, 60
maniples, 10, **11**, 14, 16, 26, 27, 39
depth of, 16
encampment of, **15**
marching, 12-13, **12**, 27, 44, 52-53, **52-53**
marines, 21, **21**, 68
Marius, 26, 27, 35
"Marius's mules", 27
market, see *forum*
mess tin, **53**
mile-castles, 57
military crowns (*coronae*), 68, **68**
Misenum, fleet at, 21
Mount of Olives, **62**, 63
Mount Scopus, **62**, 63
Mucianus, 52, 53, 55, 58, 59, 70

navy, Carthaginian, 20
Imperial, 21, 22-23
Republican, 12, 20-21, 22-23
Nero, 37, 38, 40-43, 46
Neuss, camp at, **39**, 71
Numantia, barrack blocks from, **15**
belt plates from, 50
chain from, **53**
excavations at, 9
sieges of, 33, 42
weapons from, 18, **19**, 35, 51

oars, 20, 22, 23
oath, military, 10, 44
Oberraden, *pila* from, 51, **51**
officers, military, 11, 27, 46-47, **46-47**
naval, 20-21
Olympus, Mt, 10, 13, 17
omens, 16, 20
onager, 66
optio, 11, **11**, **40**, 47
Otho, 42, 43, 45, 47, 56
outrigger, 20, 23, **23**
ovation, 71

palisade, 32, 62, 63, 66
stakes, 13, **53**
Palatine Hill, 71
parma equestris, 58, **58**
Paullus, Aemilius, 10, 16, 17, 18, 26, 33
pay, auxiliary, 55
cavalry, 59
legionary, 26, 44
praetorian, 43
Pergamum, relief from, 19, **19**
Perseus, king of Macedon, 11, 12, 18, 20, 22, 33, 71
phalanx, Macedonian, 9, **9**, 16-17
Roman, 17, **17**
phalerae, 68, **68**, **69**

pig's head, 17, **17**
pilum, 10, 16, 17, 18, 19, **19**, 26, 27, 33, 35, **35**, 50, **51**
plate armour, 48
Po, River, 27, 55, 56
helmets from, 49, **49**
Polybius, 9, 18, 22, 30, 52
camp of, 14-15, **14-15**
Pompeii, *groma* from 12, **12**
swords from, 51, **51**
Pompey the Great, 20, 58
porta praetoria, **14-15**
porta principalis, **14-15**
praefectus castrorum, 40, 46, 47
praefectus praetorio, 42
praefectus urbanus, 43
praefectus vigilum, 43
Praenestine ship, 21, **21**, 23
praetorium, 12, 14, **14-15**, 39, **39**, 42
Praetorian guard, 42-43, **42-43**, 45, 49, 52, 68
prefect, auxiliary, 52, 54
cavalry, 58
naval, 21
Republican, 11
primi ordines, 46
primus pilus, 11, **40**, 46, **46**, 47
princeps, principes, 10, **10**, 12, 14-17, 26, 27, 46
principales, 47
principia, 39, **39**, 44
prisoners, 71
punishments, 14, 69
Pydna, battle of, 9, **9**, 16-17, 18, 20, 33, 42, 58

quadrireme, 22
quaestionarii, 47
quaestorium, **14-15**
quinquereme, 20-21, **21**, 22, **22**

ram, battering, 23, 63, 66-67, **66**, 68
ram, ship's, 21, 23
ramps, 31, **31**
rampart, 32, **32**
see also camp defences
rations, 53
raven, 20, 21, 23
rearguard, 12, 52
recruits, 11, 26, 41, 44
retirement, 44
rewards, 68, **68**, 69
Rhine, 27, 28, 38, 55, 58, 71
defences, 56
fleet on, 21
river crossing, 28, 53, **53**
roads, 30, **30**
Romulus, 70
rowers, 22
rudder, 23

Sacred Island, ship from, **23**
saddles, 60-61, **61**
sails, 21, 23
sandals, 50, **50**
sash, symbol of rank, 34, **35**
scabbards, 50, **51**
Scipio, 17, 68
scorpions, **67**
scouts, 41, **41**, 52
screens, 63
scutum, see shield, legionary
Senate, 20, 28, 29, 43
Senators, 71
service, military, 26, 27
shield, auxiliary, **55**
cavalry, 58, **58**, **59**, 60
Celtic, 18, **18**

cover, **53**
legionary, oval, 10, **10**, **11**, 12, 17, 18, **18**, 26, **26**, 34, **34**, **43**
legionary, rectangular, 50, **50**
motifs, 50
officer's, 34, **35**
of *velites*, 10, **10**
siege tactics, 31, 62
towers, 23, 61, 63, **63**
weapons, 23, 52, 62, **62**, 63, **63**
works, 31, **31**, 32-33, **32-33**, 36-37
signal towers, **56**, 57
signifer, 11, **11** 40, 47, **47**
signum, 44, **45**, 58
slave legions, 10
slingers, 54, **54**
spatha, 60, **60**
spear, auxiliary, 55
cavalry, 60
silver, 68
of *triarius*, 10, **10**, 19, **19**
Sperlonga, ship from, 23, **23**
speculatores, 47
sports, cavalry, 64, 65, **64-65**
spurs, 61, **61**
stakes, palisade, 13, **53**
standard bearer, 11, 16, 47, **47**, 69
standards, legionary, 44, 45, **45**, 52
praetorian, **42**, 43
Scythian, **64**, **65**
stirrups, 44, 61
stones, catapult, 44, 66, **67**
sword, auxiliary, 55
cavalry, 60, **60**
legionary, 10, 16, 17, 26, 27, 33, 35, 50, 51, **51**
Spanish, 18, **19**, 26, 51

Tacitus, 37, 50
temple of Jerusalem, 62, 65, 67-69
tent, 12, **14**, 38, **53**
tessera, 11
tesserarius, 11, **11**, 14, **40**, 47
testudo, see tortoise
Tiberius, 48, 56
Titus, 46, 52, 63-69, 71
Arch of, **70**, **71**
Triumph of, **72-73**
tools, entrenching, **32**, 33
torques, 68, **68**, **69**
tortoise, 62, 63, **63**
ram, **66**, 67
towers, defensive, 32, **32**
siege, 31, **36-37**, 63, **63**, 65, 66, 67
for ships, 23
training, 44, **44**
Trajan, 28, 30, 37, 56, 57
Trajan's Column, 37
auxiliaries on, 54, **54**

boats on, 53
bridges on, **29**
catapult on, **67**
horsemen on, 58-59, **59**
legionary armour on, 48, **48**
ships on, **23**
soldiers marching on, 53, **53**
standards on, **45**
triarius, 10, **10**, 12, 14, 15, 16, 17, 26, 27, 47
position in camp, **14-15**
tribune, 10, 11, 12, 13, 27, **27**, 34, **34**, **35**, 47, **47**, **52**, 68
houses of, 39
tribunus angusticlavius, **40**, 47
tribunus laticlavius, **40**, 47
trierarch, 21
trireme, 21, 22
triumph, 20, 70-71, **70-71**, **72-73**
trophy, 70, **70**
trumpet, see *cornu*
trumpeter, see *cornicen*
turf cutter, **32**, 33
turma, 11, **11**, 58

urban cohorts, 43, 45

vanguard, 12, 52, **52**
Vegetius, 37, 63
veles, velites, 10, **10**, 12, 14, 26, **26**, 59
Vercingetorix, 30, 31, 32, 33, 71
Verginius, 42, 44, 45
Vespasian, 41, 42, 46, 47, **47**, 52, 54, 58, 69, 70, 71
veterans, 10, 52, 56
vexillum, 44, **45**, 58
golden, 68
via praetoria, **14-15**, 39
via principalis, **14-15**, 39
via quintana, **14-15**, 44
vigiles, 43
Vindex, 40, 41
vineae, see galleries
Vitellius, Aulus, 42, 45, 47, 52-57, 59, 70, 71
Vitruvius, 63, 66

weapons, auxiliary, 55, **55**
cavalry, 60, **60**
Caesarian, 60, **60**
Imperial, 51, **51**
Republican, 10, 18-19, **19**
Spanish, 18-19, **19**
training, 44
workshops, 38, 39, **39**
wreath, laurel, 70, 71
myrtle, 71

Zama, battle of, 17

Metric Conversion Table

10 millimetres = 0.39 inches
20 millimetres = 0.78 inches
30 millimetres = 1.18 inches

1 metre	=	3.28 feet
50 metres	=	164.04 feet
100 metres	=	328.08 feet

1 kilometre = 0.62 miles